P9-CRH-865

Praise for Elizabeth Catte's
What You Are Getting Wrong About Appalachia:

"Small presses across Appalachia and the Rust Belt consistently publish, to little fanfare, incredibly diverse work—books that are lush, gritty, surprising and so very true. Perhaps the best example, or certainly the best place to begin, is Catte's *What You Are Getting Wrong About Appalachia.* This edgy, meticulous work of nonfiction from Cleveland's Belt Publishing dispels many myths about the region."
—Leah Hampton, *Los Angeles Times*

"Catte's slim, very readable volume is like a more focused version of Howard Zinn's venerable *A People's History Of The United States*, turning its lens to the on-the-ground civic struggles of people who have lived and died in Appalachia."—**Laura Adamczyk, *The A.V. Club***

"A brief, forceful, and necessary correction."
—Frank Guan, *Bookforum*

"You couldn't kill this book with a hammer. Come and watch Elizabeth Catte clip the hollow wings of little jimmy vance. Stay and behold an enlightened vision, a living solidarity found among the strong and varied peoples of this misunderstood land."—**Glenn Taylor, author of *The Ballad of Trenchmount Taggart***

"What are we getting wrong about Appalachia? A lot. . . . This is a necessary antidote to the cyclical mainstream interest in Appalachia as a backwards, white working-class caricature."—**Tressie McMillan Cottom, author of *Thick***

"A bold refusal to submit to stereotype."—*Kirkus Reviews*

"Succeeds in providing a richer, more complex view of a much-maligned region."—*Publishers Weekly*

PURE
AMERICA

Eugenics and the Making of Modern Virginia

Elizabeth Catte

Belt Publishing

Printed in the United States of America
First edition 2021
1 2 3 4 5 6 7 8 9

ISBN: 978-1-948742-73-3

Belt Publishing
5322 Fleet Avenue
Cleveland, Ohio 44105
www.beltpublishing.com

Cover art by David Wilson
Book design by Meredith Pangrace

TABLE OF CONTENTS

A NOTE ON LANGUAGE AND CONTENT

This book repeats some ugly and abusive language that historical actors invented to describe people perceived to have disabilities in the past. Much of this language is specific to the outlook held by physicians, lawmakers, and laypeople who lived in the early twentieth century. In this period, labels such as "feebleminded," "unfit," and "defective" had clinical understandings, but these terms were also applied broadly and in derogatory ways to describe people with presumed shortcomings of character. In many examples that appear in this book, historical actors used their language of disability to describe people that we would not consider disabled today.

In *No Right to Be Idle: The Invention of Disability 1840s–1930s*, historian Sarah F. Rose writes, "the experience of disability, and even what counts as a disability, varies by historical era and culture. The ways in which race, class, gender, age, and kind of impairment . . . intersect with disability also matter, of course." In some contexts, it is relevant to emphasize that many of the victims of eugenics and forced sterilization were not disabled according to our contemporary use of the term. But capturing the ways that perceptions of disabilities shift with time and place does not mean the primary injustice of eugenics was that it ensnared so-called "normal people." Rather, the shifting nature of these perceptions and the realities that followed underscore that there is a long history in America of imprinting racial, gender, and class prejudices onto the concept of disability.

For readers who want more information about these ideas, including the ways that they continue to circulate today, there is a list of suggested resources at the back of this book.

INTRODUCTION

This is a book about eugenics, which is to say it is a book about my neighborhood.

When I started writing *Pure America*, I lived on one of the more elevated streets in Staunton, Virginia, a small city nestled in the Shenandoah Valley. For years, my daily routine played out in exactly the same way: I'd leave my apartment, coast down the hill a quarter of a mile toward Richmond Avenue, Staunton's main thoroughfare, and catch a traffic light that put me nose to nose with the original campus of Western State Hospital, where, between 1927 and 1964, surgeons sterilized around 1,700 people without their consent.

When I describe the hospital like that, you might conjure up an image of my daily commute that seems ripped from the mind of Shirley Jackson: *Western State, not sane, stood by itself against the hills, holding darkness within.* But instead, what I came nose to nose with every day was a bustling construction project. The site—an assembly of buildings and land, including a cemetery that contains the remains of as many as 3,000 former patients—was being diligently transformed into a luxury hotel and an upscale property development marketed to retirees and second-home buyers.

In other words, Western State did not stand by itself at all. It was open for business, undergoing renovations that would soon turn it into the newly christened Blackburn Inn and the Villages at Staunton. Its new charm included the meticulous restoration of some of the site's key architectural structures, but also a branding identity that claimed Western State was the home of an oddly cheerful history: patients who were well-cared-for by benevolent, moral physicians. When you heard the developers' historical account of the hospital, which had originally been named the Western State Lunatic Asylum, the place felt so sumptuous that you wondered why people in the past didn't feign insanity just for a chance to visit.

This was not the Western State Hospital that I knew.

A period of what is sometimes called "moral medicine" did indeed briefly exist there, from its opening in 1828 to just after the Civil War. In its earliest and more optimistic configuration, Western State provided respite for white patients who were experiencing acute distress that physicians thought could be relieved by rest, proper nutrition, and a routine of light work. This more humane treatment, the "moral" in moral medicine, was intended to help individuals "regain" their sanity in peaceful environments by setting aside methods such as restraint and corporal punishment that a new generation of physicians felt were unnecessary and brutal. In this period, individuals with more severe, incurable, or chronic conditions, both mental and physical, were cared for by their families ideally, sometimes with assistance from charities, or they were placed by communities or their kin in locally funded almshouses, orphanages, or jails.

But in the late nineteenth and early twentieth centuries, that approach was supplanted by a long era in the history of psychiatric medicine when therapeutic efforts primarily focused on containment and control, not care or cure. More and more, people perceived to have disabilities, along with those who couldn't care for themselves due to poverty or age, were viewed by society as an expensive and disorderly class prone to criminal behaviors and indigence. Communities began to demand financial relief from the costs associated with helping them survive. By institutionalizing individuals in greater numbers, communities could pass their local financial costs to the state and rid themselves of people who were thought to lead unproductive lives. According to legal scholar Laura Appleman, by 1923 more than 263,000 people were institutionalized nationwide, which meant that "The first modern mass incarceration was not of criminal offenders, but of the disabled."

Physicians and scientists abandoned their search for moral treatment and instead turned their efforts to prevention by quantifying and categorizing, with ever greater precision, the types and causes of what they considered to be mental incompetence. Their studies, helped by the invention of intelligence testing, produced new taxonomies of weakness, but they overwhelmingly agreed that these afflictions all had a similar root cause: bad breeding.

This was a problem involving both biology and economics. In addition to diagnosing their patients, physicians began enumerating the financial burden and social dangers associated with their survival. Proponents of a rapidly growing movement to study and control human breeding found the pressure point of a unifying message: allowing the "unfit" to reproduce was tantamount to creating a societal debt that could never be repaid. "Every 15 seconds 100 dollars of your money goes to the care of persons with bad heredity: the insane, feebleminded, criminals and other defectives," read one series of advertisements circulated by the American Eugenics Society in the 1920s. Virginia made eugenic sterilization legal in 1924.

The Western State that I knew was largely a product of this longer historical era. The hospital's superintendent from 1905 to 1943 was such a vocal leader of Virginia's eugenics movement that people knew him as Joseph "Sterilization" DeJarnette. He was one of the state's earliest proponents of population control, calling for marriage restrictions for the "unfit" in 1908. By 1911, he was recommending the sterilization of "all weaklings." After Virginia passed its Sterilization Act in 1924, and it was affirmed by the Supreme Court in 1927, DeJarnette and the surgeons who worked under him at Western State performed the second-highest number of sterilization procedures in

Virginia. Only the Lynchburg Colony, seventy-five miles to the south and designed specifically for feebleminded patients, outpaced it.

Western State remained a segregated hospital reserved for white patients until Virginia was forced to integrate facilities after 1965. Eastern State Hospital in Williamsburg, opened in 1773 as the first public hospital in the United States designed solely for the treatment of mental illness, functioned briefly as an integrated hospital between 1841 and 1870 (with a segregated basement wing for Black patients). After it reverted to a segregated facility for white patients, Eastern State performed 393 sterilizations between 1924 and 1964. In 1869, Virginia opened the Central Lunatic Asylum for Colored Insane in Petersburg, another first of its kind in the United States. It, along with its smaller Petersburg Colony, remained Virginia's only facilities for Black patients until after integration. Central State performed 1,634 sterilizations, and the Petersburg Colony, which closed in 1955, performed 246. Virginia operated an additional facility for white patients near Marion as the Southwestern Lunatic Asylum, opened in 1887. Around 364 sterilizations were performed there between 1924 and 1964. The Lynchburg Colony, dating to 1910 and where the state confined many but not all white patients labeled feebleminded, performed at least 2,781 sterilization procedures.

Earlier in my life, I lived outside of Nashville among plantations, not hospitals. There my neighbor was enslavement, not eugenics. I am telling you this because when I first moved to Staunton, Western State froze me in a sense of *déjà vu*; I was again encountering local historical narratives that were dominated by people who were happy, yet forcibly detained, and fine architecture, instead of by trauma and corporeal violence. Enslavement is not eugenics, and yet the two felt familiar, as if all of those modern-day plantation weddings and antebellum architectural distractions had helped lead to a point where this deeply complicated site in Staunton had similarly turned into a valuable asset that was economically inseparable from the modern growth of the community around it.

Were the cheerful stories the developers were telling about Western State intended to achieve some kind of historical balance? Were they meant to help the site and the community move beyond the stigma of eugenics? Or was this more anodyne history just designed to please wealthy property owners and visitors who wanted to stay there? The transformed Western State Hospital boasted new numbers city residents could celebrate: a $21 million investment from developers, $1.2 million in tax credits from the state and federal government, and $595,000 properties for sale. But there were other numbers from its past that now felt unseemly to say out loud: 1,700 lives altered, thousands of graves.

"But the site has good bones," I heard people in town say, praising Western State's architectural pedigree and thinking charitably about the transformations and profits still to come. Poet Maggie Smith tells us:

Any decent realtor,
walking you through a real shithole, chirps on
about good bones: This place could be beautiful,
right? You could make this place beautiful.

Well, this is a book about being uncharitable.

Pure America is a history of Virginia's eugenics movement, including the role Western State Hospital played in it. But it is also about the way I see that history in the built world and natural environment I experience every day. My regular encounters with Western State helped me realize in a visceral way that eugenics didn't just alter the lives of people, it also altered land and geography. It changed how institutions grew, and it gave Virginians confidence that they could claim the physical world just as readily as they claimed the bodies of its citizens. These alterations also produced assets and provided convenient ways to mark geographies as pure or unpure. All of these changes had economic implications, and they're intimately tied into very real profits and losses in the present.

But the world described in this book is simply the world of my daily commute. On many days, I make my way east from Staunton for a forty-mile trek to Charlottesville. That journey takes me past Western State, through the mountains, past the southern entrance to Shenandoah National Park, and into a city that is inseparable from the University of Virginia. These are my landscapes, each of them different in terms of their physical environment and the layers of this story they can reveal.

Charlottesville, for example, was home to Carrie Buck, who was the central figure in *Buck v. Bell*, the 1927 Supreme Court case that legalized eugenic sterilization nationwide. Raped by her foster mother's nephew, Carrie was institutionalized so her foster family could avoid the scandal of her pregnancy. She eventually became the first person legally sterilized in Virginia. I often drive past the cemetery where she is buried and through the neighborhood where she lived before her commitment to what was then called the Virginia State Colony for Epileptics and Feebleminded in Lynchburg. I take this route because it's the most convenient way to get to Charlottesville's downtown mall, where my partner Josh works.

That mall is still marked by the efforts white citizens made to claim territory for themselves during the eugenics era. In 1921 and 1924, city residents placed two large Confederate statues here. Almost a hundred years later, those same statues served as the focal points of violence during 2017's Unite the Right rally. The University of Virginia, about a mile to the west, participated heavily in the pageantry that accompanied the statues' original placements. In the early twentieth century, the university also functioned as an academic larder well-stocked with eugenicists, an institution described by current UVA history professor Elizabeth Varon as "an incubator for Lost Cause ideology." Ambitious white faculty, eager to enhance their reputations, claimed as scientific law the truth of their own genetic perfection and taught students who would go on to populate Virginia's highest political offices, the medical field, and the law.

The area's surrounding mountains, both the ones I see during my commute and the ones that greet me as more distant landscapes when I arrive back home, were prized by Virginia's earliest psychiatrists, who believed natural beauty could soothe troubled minds. But twentieth-century eugenicists also saw them as sinister geographies crawling with people they thought of as "mongrels." My commute runs right past a turnoff for Shenandoah National Park. Since 1935, the park has been one of the most robust drivers of regional tourism, but that success was achieved through the removal of 500 mountain families through a new form of eviction—eminent domain—that Virginia used to ease the process. The sweeping laws the state passed in 1928 to help the park's development set in motion a chain reaction that brought more and more people to the mountains to determine what should happen to families too poor to leave the park on their own. For some, what would happen were institutions like Western State and the Lynchburg Colony.

I've tried to understand how all these locations that punctuate my commute—places of violence, racial supremacy, and displacement—connect to the layers of history in Western State's past. In Staunton and at the renovated hospital, questions of profit and loss are always in the foreground. The city's local economy is not only reliant on tourism connected to the surrounding mountains, but also on its ability to project a wholesome, historic image. Boosters argue we've earned the ability to move beyond the city's darker chapters. But what does it mean when the local economy is still extracting profit from them?

Looking at eugenics through the variation of landscapes and their economies has helped me understand how acolytes of eugenics moved through a similar constellation of ideas even while their primary motivations and targets were different. For some, eugenics was part of an unrelenting campaign of white supremacy. For others, it was a partial solution to control "troublesome" women. For many, it was a more ambiguous and opportunistic tool that helped elite Virginians extract profits or take assets from poor people by arguing for the biological truth of their unworthiness.

Like geographies, these motivations aren't seamless. They aren't always easy to locate either. They are everywhere, but because eugenics is best understood through the history of ideas and not places, they are also nowhere at all. How could it be that I live at the epicenter of Virginia's eugenics movement and see almost nothing around me today that tells that story? From that paradox, *Pure America* was born.

I don't want to give the impression, however, that *Pure America* is a secret history of anything. "Virginia Ran a Secret Eugenics Program that Didn't End Until 1979," an article on *Medium* tells me. *Nature* calls it "America's Hidden History." The *New Yorker* encourages us to remember "The Forgotten Lessons of the Eugenics Movement." In Virginia, just like the rest of the world, these facts of history haven't been forgotten. It's just that powerful people have oriented the past around stories they feel are more important to tell.

This may sound like a subtle difference, but I assure you it is not. Forgetting is passive, organic, even gentle at times. Intentionally crowding a collective history with elements that are specifically designed to ease discomfort or conceal controversy is active, intentional, coercive.

My ability to discover evidence of Virginia's eugenic past in the landscape of my daily life was buttressed by my background as a historian, someone supposedly trained to look at the past accurately and call it for what it really was. But in spite of that training, in Staunton I felt a familiar pull. Wouldn't it feel better just to give in and only think about the hospital through stories about happy patients and beautiful architecture? After all, the old version of the site didn't tell stories at all. It was just a derelict collection of buildings. Would it really be so terrible to put them to new use? Wouldn't it be better to have something there instead of nothing?

Arguments like these were familiar to me, and these questions are far from settled, even among people who have spent their entire careers thinking about them. But what I can tell you is that the current reconfiguration of Western State started to make me feel what historian Kate Brown describes when she writes, "at some point even the wreckage progress leaves in its wake becomes profitable." When we recover some stories about the past and set aside others, we are often placing real, material value on those stories. Even if some questions remain unsettled, an acknowledgement of this truth is required. Now, because of my inability to let go of Western State's past, the site makes me feel like I have failed to be a good member of my community who is invested in its economic future. That is often what I hate most about it.

Calling Virginia's eugenic past a secret history also runs contrary to the work of important scholars who have already written extensively about the eugenics movement and its connected goals. One of those scholars was my dissertation adviser, Pippa Holloway, whose book *Sexuality, Politics, and Social Control in Virginia, 1920–1945* follows the state's attempts to regulate the sexual behavior of its "undesirable" citizens. Katrina Powell and Sue Currell have researched and written about the displacement of families at the Shenandoah National Park. Two of the country's leading experts on American eugenics, Paul Lombardo and Gregory Michael Dorr, began their careers by making Virginia's past their primary subject. Dorr's account, *Segregation's Science*, was the first book I reread when I moved to Staunton and felt my mind starting to slip. I began asking people, "That's *the* Western State, right?" as if there might be another former asylum in town that hadn't become $500,000 condominiums.

These scholars, and many others, have examined eugenics from the perspective of law, policy, and science. They've written about it as a set of ideas and an extension of state bureaucracies. In two cases, their work has even helped create compensation programs for victims of eugenic sterilization. North Carolina created the first program in 2013, due in part to historian Johanna Schoen's work on the state's Eugenics Board, and Virginia enacted a similar program in 2015. Victim advocacy by disability and reproductive rights activists also helped create these and other measures, like the repeal of state laws that permitted eugenic sterilization well into the twenty-first century. But despite all of this work, as a nation we are still coming to terms with the legacy of eugenics, even though its origins and early applications are well-documented. Its legacy still exists in our current immigration laws and our for-profit health care system. It underlies our fascination with mail-in DNA tests and ancestry. It informs the rhetoric politicians use to talk about public assistance. Just as it was in the past, eugenics is everywhere and nowhere at the same time.

It just depends on how much we're willing to interrogate how power works in the world we live in today.

If the history of eugenics does have an element of secrecy, though, it's this: sterilization statistics can be finicky, and it is not uncommon to read minor variations in reported numbers depending on the source, its purpose, or when it was produced. I tend to rely on Gregory Dorr's work for statistics during the eugenics movement in terms of operations performed and breakdowns according to gender and race. But it is important to note that individual patient records, even those of patients who are long dead, are still protected by medical privacy laws. It's likely that Virginia buried patients anonymously at Western State, for example, using only numbered markers, precisely for this reason.

But the majority of my archival sources are housed at the Library of Virginia in Richmond and the University of Virginia Special Collections in Charlottesville, places that aren't secret at all. For the most part, the only credential I needed to access this information was an ordinary Virginia library card. When you hear the phrase "secret eugenics program," it conjures up images of someone furtively fingering through file boxes in a basement while someone else watches the door. But the process really just involved me sitting in a comfortable room while the on-duty archivist retrieved files that had been meticulously arranged by thousands of hours of labor.

So please, I am not here to reveal secrets. What I want to do instead is give Virginia's eugenic past a sense of place and bring it home, to find it like the faint pencil mark in a childhood closet that recorded how small you once were.

Here is something about this book that might get me into trouble: I think most eugenicists were bad people. There will be no "man of his time" hedging here. In Staunton, for example, DeJarnette, to the extent that his legacy is acknowledged at all, is often contextualized today as a person with flawed but "deeply humanitarian motives." That's how the local newspaper remembered him in 2014, the same year Virginia lawmakers sought to compel the state to authorize reparations for survivors of eugenic sterilization. "Letters to DeJarnette filed in the state archives show writers from many social ranks relating to him with high personal and professional regard." This was a man who wrote poems musing whether or not Black people (although he didn't call them that) should be allowed into heaven.

When people today try to contextualize figures like DeJarnette this way, I know what they're trying to do. They mean that these beliefs about good breeding and racial supremacy were endorsed by a critical mass of white leaders and intelligentsia. They were ingrained to such an extent that we might call them "typical" when we're trying to determine how powerful people during this era thought the world should work.

But what would the people who were targeted by eugenics say? Are we implying that the record number of immigrants ensnared by these beliefs would be comforted by the fact that history would eventually prove that they weren't of a different species? No. Did elderly women and men cope with their forced childlessness by understanding that doctors had tried their best but simply got it wrong? Again, no. What those people would say, and what they have said, is that nothing about what was done to them made any sense. If some of us are able to make sense of it now, because it did not happen to us, then that is a gift. But it does not grant us permission to build a legacy on a series of excuses.

I will not be scolded for imagining men like Joseph DeJarnette, Walter Plecker, Aubrey Strode, or George Pollock in the way I understand them, as individuals who derived status and pleasure from the power they wielded over vulnerable people. I do not care if someone accuses me of the ultimate historical sin of *judging people in the past by the yardstick of the present.* I do not subscribe to the view that time is the real villain of this story, that it tormented important people with difficult questions—like what the cheapest way was to castrate a prisoner—that only an accident of fate forced them to answer.

Eugenics made a mask from the newness of things; from the power to transform old evils into modern interventions. To use a more locally inspired turn of phrase, eugenics painted fresh white columns on an old building filled with shit and sold it. After all, it had good bones.

Lurking beneath the sound and fury of the eugenics movement and its language of defectives, mongrels, and misfits is a set of brutal yet recognizable beliefs about the kind of lives people on the margins deserve. Thinking of eugenics more broadly as a world-building enterprise has helped me understand how a quest for economic purity was just as important to eugenicists as racial and genetic purity were. Early twentieth-century eugenicists argued for the elimination of the unfit based on what they saw as the group's potential to siphon resources away from the more deserving and to transmit debts onto future generations. If the eugenicists were successful, they figured the rate of return on their actions would be enormous. It would relieve the burden on prisons, institutions, and welfare offices and end the need to help engineer the survival of people who had no right to be alive and yet were.

Often, when we talk about eugenics now, even when we are attentive to the lives of the people it ensnared, we emphasize that this was the world that eugenicists were *trying* to create. Eugenics itself provides the framework for this perspective; it was always building toward a future goal. Sometimes for our own comfort, we also emphasize the failure of eugenicists. We understand their beliefs endured in some way—in debates about welfare mothers, immigrants from shithole countries, or work requirements for public aid recipients, for example. But as Audrey Farley writes in her essay about the cultural legacy of the eugenics movement, a tendency remains to "situate eugenics in the remote past." That emphasis on remoteness, on the ways eugenicists *tried but failed*, sometimes obscures a way of seeing the world they actually made and how it lives on in the present.

For many people, the endurance of those beliefs is what matters. I hope this book shows how real and physical that endurance can be. In showing you the map of my world, I also want to show you how you might make your own. As Muriel Rukeyser puts it in *The Book of the Dead*, "These roads will take you into your own country."

This book is about what was taken and how it helped build the world around me, in Staunton and beyond. It is also about the wealth and power that still circulate through that world-building endeavor. It is a book about imagining eugenics as it still exists in sites like Western State Hospital, thrumming in place like Rilke's torso of Apollo: "still suffused with brilliance from inside, / like a lamp, in which his gaze, now turned to low, / gleams in all its power."

"This is a story within a story," I tell myself. And this is how it starts.

CHAPTER ONE:

MOTHERS AND DAUGHTERS

Wand you stand in Charlottesville's Oakwood Cemetery beside the grave of the woman buried as Carrie Detamore, but who was better known as Carrie Buck, your surroundings will tell you a story. Find its beginning in the places you need not go; in a concrete-choked field you visit as an unwelcome guest, in grasslands dotted with the smallest possible proof of death. That you are standing in a city cemetery and not a pauper's field means that Carrie did not die in an institution, and therefore wasn't buried where she was confined, like her mother Emma was. There's no way you could know this, but I'll tell you: Carrie Detamore was seventy-four years old the last time she visited her mother's grave at the former Virginia State Colony for Epileptics and Feebleminded. I did the math backward from the day social workers took Carrie to see the building where she herself had been sterilized fifty-seven years earlier and she collapsed at the sight of it.

Not far from Carrie's grave is a plot dedicated to the Dobbs family. After the state removed Carrie from her mother's care when she was around four years old, John and Alice Dobbs became her foster parents. At least that's how the courts described them. In reality, Carrie was the Dobbses' housekeeper. But what was the difference between being a ward of the state and being a maid? Everyone said poor girls needed to work harder than hard. It would teach them important lessons.

Here is the lesson that Carrie learned, first from John

and Alice Dobbs and then the Supreme Court: that a man can rape you and you will be punished for it, disappeared to the same place that swallowed your mother. When she was seventeen years old, Carrie was raped by Clarence Garland, Alice Dobbs's nephew, and she became pregnant. Looking to avoid a scandal, the Dobbses soon discovered that in Virginia in 1924, it was as easy to commit a poor young woman to an institution as it was to make her a maid at the age of ten. John and Alice initially pretended Carrie was epileptic; a logical if not dishonest strategy meant to make her seem suited for an institution called the Colony for Epileptics and Feebleminded. But there was no need to pretend. As a poor, white girl from a bad family, Carrie's admission criterion was simply who she was—the product and the carrier of bad genes.

When I visit Oakwood Cemetery now, I never stop by the grave of Alice Dobbs. I don't like wondering what she found more upsetting; that her nephew had raped Carrie, or that in hiding the resulting pregnancy, she had to lose her housekeeper?

After Carrie was committed to the Lynchburg Colony, her life eventually became a matter of law. Virginia used her to make its case that the state's Sterilization Act, passed in 1924, could withstand constitutional scrutiny. "If sterilized under law," the state argued, "she could be given her liberty and secure a good home, under supervision, without injury to society." Sterilization would make Carrie safer to the people around her, the argument went. But it would also make her a better worker; no more children to interrupt her productivity. The Supreme Court agreed in 1927. "Three generations of imbeciles are enough," Justice Oliver Wendell Holmes, Jr decreed, later boasting in private letters of his "brutal" affirming opinion.

Standing in Oakwood Cemetery at Carrie's grave reveals a truth that is both profound and difficult to imagine: that she survived, and her life was long. Carrie died in 1983. But what was that life like? Just weeks after her operation, she began working at a lumber mill under the supervision of the Lynchburg Colony. That supervision continued when she next worked as a maid. A husband came, then died. Then Carrie married again. There were little gardens, pigs, and reunions with siblings she thought she had lost.

In the Dobbs family plot, there is a little marker that bears the initials VAED. This is Carrie's daughter, Vivian. After they committed Carrie to the Lynchburg Colony, the Dobbses adopted Vivian, most likely out of guilt or embarrassment. By virtue of her biological mother and grandmother, the Supreme Court labeled Vivian an "illegitimate, feebleminded child" from birth. She died of colitis when she was eight years old, the phantom third generation of a family of imbeciles who were never imbeciles at all. They were just poor.

Soon after Carrie's death, legal scholar Paul Lombardo tracked down Vivian's report cards from the Venable Public Elementary School in Charlottesville. Her scholastic record shows achievements in many subjects, a remarkable feat for a young woman most assuredly raised in a home where she was seen as a burden.

Seventy-five years after the Supreme Court sealed Carrie's fate, the state of Virginia placed a historical marker near the Venable School. It reads:

> In 1924, Virginia, like a majority of states then, enacted eugenic sterilization laws. Virginia's law allowed state institutions to operate on individuals to prevent the conception of what were believed to be "genetically inferior" children. Charlottesville native Carrie Buck (1906–1983), involuntarily committed to a state facility near Lynchburg, was chosen as the first person to be sterilized under

the new law. The U. S. Supreme Court, in *Buck v. Bell*, on 2 May 1927, affirmed the Virginia law. After Buck more than 8,000 other Virginians were sterilized before the most relevant parts of the act were repealed in 1974. Later evidence eventually showed that Buck and many others had no "hereditary defects." She is buried south of here.

If you raise your eyes from Carrie's grave to the hill above it, you might catch the sun glinting off the dark glass and light stone of new homes. Locals will recognize the signature architectural style of Charlottesville's modern builds; three or four stories of boxy, fresh narrowness, plotted out as neatly as the cemetery below them. The ones in direct view from Carrie's grave are priced at $500,000.

Their close proximity to the old cemetery might seem odd, but I can easily explain it: Charlottesville is running out of space to build new homes because the zoning laws it once relied on to keep Black people out of white neighborhoods are now inhibiting the city's ability to grow. As useable land becomes scarcer, a millionaire's house atop a cemetery is not such a strange thing. But where does everyone else go?

Standing in that cemetery now, you might hope that the Charlottesville of today is different than the place Carrie Buck was born into in 1906. But the surroundings here will tell you that things haven't changed at all. Here is the lesson that we will learn from Carrie, a quirk of fate communicated accidentally but clearly by the geography of this small corner of the city: at the top are the rich, at the bottom the poor, and despite any sentiments to the contrary, the two will never be equal, not even in death.

Eugenics is a set of scientific and philosophical beliefs aimed at breeding better humans. Much like a farmer calibrates his stock through selective breeding and culling, eugenics brought the sensibilities of the barnyard into the bedroom.

The birth of eugenics had many midwives. Sir Francis Galton, a statistician, inventor, and cousin of Charles Darwin, coined the term in 1883 and helped provide a new language for the debate over a question that had been simmering for a long time, first in England and then in America: why was there such a pronounced difference between the upper and lower classes? Galton argued that the stuff of genius likely ran in families and within bloodlines. This was not an earth-shattering proposition for a member of the aristocratic class to make. What made Galton different, though, was his suggestion that this genius could be quantified and tracked with scientific precision.

Then, at the turn of the twentieth century, the scientific world rediscovered the work of a nineteenth-century friar named Gregor Mendel. What we now called Mendel's Laws of Inheritance proposed that humans could predict the inheritance of traits from parents to offspring. Through the work of later scientists, the qualities Mendel called "factors" became "genes," and Galton's acolytes were able to extend his original theories into areas that his own genius could not reach at first, including how his ideas about families and bloodlines could work in practice.

Mendel's Laws empowered a growing contingent of scientists, mostly biologists and agriculturalists—the breeders of things—to further their case that it was genetic failure, not the environment, that was the primary cause of undesirable individual and social outcomes. Charles Davenport, a Harvard-trained biologist, was one of the most influential members of this cohort. In 1904, he became director of the Carnegie Institution's Cold Spring Harbor Laboratory in

New York. The lab had been created to study heredity in plants and animals, but Davenport quickly reoriented it to study human inheritance. He first used Mendelian genetics to explore visible traits like eye and skin color, but soon, he and his wife Gertrude found much more subjective territory to explore, like the inheritance of temperament, musical aptitude, athletic ability, and "mental peculiarities."

There's an air of competition in the early work of eugenicists as each tried to outdo the other by finding the most "deranged" families to test their theories. Their studies were often nothing more than highly fictionalized worlds populated by, in Davenport's words, "alcoholic harlots," "licentious women," and "unambitious, disorderly men." In contrast, eugenicists thought of themselves as racehorses; hard-working animals at the peak of fitness who would sire the next generation of societal winners. In *White Trash: The 400-Year Untold Story of Class in America*, historian Nancy Isenberg writes, "Almost as a mantra, eugenicists compared good human stock to thoroughbreds, equating the wellborn with superior ability and inherited fitness." Today, some of Donald Trump's self-appraisals mirror the language of what is sometimes called "racehorse theory." "I had a good gene pool, so I was pretty much driven," he says in a compilation video of his best "good genes" clips on *Time*'s website.

In 1910, Davenport and his colleagues formed the Eugenics Record Office as an extension of the Cold Spring Harbor Laboratory. These enterprises were all funded by tycoon families like the Rockefellers, Carnegies, Kelloggs, and Harrimans, who believed their wealth should be put to the service of solving social problems, instead of simply recirculating as charity (or adequate wages for the workers in their industries). The following year, Davenport completed *Heredity in Relation to Eugenics*, which argued, "Man is an organism—an animal; and the laws of improvement of corn and race horses hold true for him also. Unless people accept this simple truth and let it influence marriage selection, human progress will cease."

Davenport intended his work to appeal to his own scientific community, his rich funders, and the American public alike by framing eugenics as a participatory science that was open to "the thousands of intelligent Americans who love the truth," as he wrote in *Heredity in Relation to Eugenics*. Ordinary Americans might participate by filling out genetic questionnaires sent out by the Eugenics Record Office to compile national data. They could also help out by supporting the government in its efforts to stop the reproduction of "defectives and delinquents." "Everyone can share in the eugenics movement," Davenport promised, and the Eugenics Record Office would continue under this steam, acting as a nerve center for a national movement until its closure in 1939.

Eugenics had both positive and negative iterations. These terms are not moral descriptors, but pragmatic ones. Positive eugenics encompassed strategies that encouraged reproduction among what the philosophy's adherents considered good genetic specimens. For example, human livestock competitions called "better baby contests" encouraged families to bring their little ones to state fairs to be judged according to newly devised standards for child development. But positive eugenics occurred in more subtle forms as well. During the New Deal, for example, the government placed eugenicists in agencies that evaluated people for new forms of social assistance, like subsidized housing. Fitter families often received the new state-funded privileges.

Negative eugenics, on the other hand, described strategies that were used to restrict reproduction. Sterilization became a favored strategy, but before it was legal, eugenicists also relied on the long-term, state-mandated confinement of "unfit" women throughout their childbearing years as a way to restrict unwanted reproduction. Eventually, however, the costs associated with long-term confinement helped elicit support for sterilization. Immigration restrictions were also regularly used as a form of negative eugenics. In 1920, the Eugenics Record Office appealed to Congress to curtail immigration in order to protect the nation's gene pool. Congress responded with sweeping immigration reforms in 1924 that blocked all immigration from Asia and established a quota system intended to significantly disadvantage southern and eastern European immigrants. Today, the United States is straining to return to a hard-line immigration system for a president who pouted in 2018, "Why are we having all these people from shithole countries come here?"

James Bowman, professor emeritus at the Pritzker School of Medicine in Chicago, argues that "passive eugenics" might also be a useful category for describing other methods that are closer to us in time. These often come under the guise of limiting resources, and they overwhelmingly reduce the quality of life for low-income people and are often racially motivated. In Bowman's model, for example, a system of for-profit medicine and the constant reduction in funding for programs that help keep poor people healthy are forms of passive eugenics. "Indirect and direct coercion in health and life insurance and employment is an almost inevitable path to cryptic eugenics," he writes.

Because the philosophies of eugenics prioritized state control at the expense of personal choice, its most common strategies did not include contraception or abortion. It would have horrified eugenicists to imagine that their ambitions of improving the human race might be at the mercy of the individual desires or needs of women (both poor and wealthy). Today, when Clarence Thomas compares modern advocates for safe abortion to eugenicists of the past, he is wrong. The most critical elements of negative eugenic strategies always relied, and still do, on top-down control over entire populations.

Why eugenics became overwhelmingly popular at the turn of the twentieth century, and what that popularity looked like in Virginia specifically, are two separate, but related, questions.

In America, the early twentieth century was a time of state building and problem solving. A run-of-the-mill history textbook would call it the Progressive Era, a historical period known for producing few winners and many losers. It was a time of monopolies and robber barons, of America pumping blood through the heart of a machine. It was an era that knew *How the Other Half Lives* and that found itself in *The Jungle*. It was a time of unprecedented immigration, of Lewis Hine photographing five-year-old workers in textile mills, and of Ida B. Wells weeping over Thomas Moss, dead at the hands of a Memphis lynch mob.

More broadly, the Progressive Era was a time when America became fully industrialized. A desire to reinvent and embrace new modern sciences and technologies carried across a range of enterprises. Typical examples of this include the changing nature of work and the invention of cheap, mass-produced goods. The factory owner and the industrialist replaced the merchant and farmer as dominant economic actors. But the lives of workers, not to mention those who couldn't work, became less valuable than the goods they produced. Reformers looked out into their cities and saw a world consumed by poverty, disease, and crime. Many tried to intervene by offering charity or advice about health and hygiene, but their efforts were like trying to write on running water. Some people began to think that it might not be society that was failing the poor, but the poor who were failing society.

Between 1880 and 1930, approximately twenty-eight million immigrants also arrived in America. The largest numbers came from countries in eastern and southern Europe to settle in already overcrowded cities. Anti-immigrant crusaders saw these groups as "alien in blood, in language, and in political, and social tradition," as Yale professor William Blackman argued in 1902. This scourge, nativists like Blackman insisted, would weaken America in every capacity by adding to its growing underclass. It would tax the limits of the country's poorhouses, take jobs from citizens, and even contaminate it from within by spreading defective genes.

Some reformers even diagnosed an alarming reversal of evolutionary progress. The unfit, they claimed, were surviving at the expense of the fittest—an entirely invented trend that sociologist Edward A. Ross in 1901 called "race suicide." In this formulation, society had reached its breaking point, and undesirables were outpopulating productive, white citizens. Every day their numbers continued to grow as more of them arrived by birth and through immigration. In their wake came the chaos of poverty, disease, and crime. And turn of the century America, which had grown so inhospitable that good families were even beginning to eliminate themselves, was only a preview of the horror that would eventually arrive. Without collective action, experts like Ross warned, degeneracy would find its way deep into the American bloodstream, and the human race would be stuck on an atavistic track that could only move backward.

Out of this dark vision, however, a ray of optimism emerged: if modernity had helped to create this problem, it might also be able to produce its solution. And so began America's quest to become a nation of better animals.

As Charles Davenport hoped, the nation embraced eugenics as a tool for social betterment to a staggering degree. Eugenics soothed American anxieties by promising that social sickness, like ordinary diseases, could be cured. The number of patients suffering from it could be reduced. Throughout the early twentieth century, Americans celebrated eugenics at state fairs, participated in fitter family contests, and watched feature films that had eugenic themes. Hundreds of universities across the country trained the next generation of physicians and social workers with scientific curricula based on eugenics. The vast majority of people who embraced eugenics in this way were white, but some Black leaders saw utility in its principles too, if for no other reason than to learn a language that was necessary to speak to their white contemporaries.

In Virginia specifically, these ambitions about social uplift were intimately tied to larger ideas about Southern uplift as well. How could Virginia's white reformers assist the collective effort to recuperate Southern identity while at the same time demonstrating they had left their brutal past behind? This was a fragile question, not least of all because this abandonment of the past was largely a cosmetic endeavor. Embracing eugenics, as Gregory Dorr argues, allowed Virginia's leaders to have the best of both worlds. The philosophy's racist and sexist underpinnings complemented a social hierarchy that they felt should be preserved, but the fact that eugenics would allow their efforts to be viewed as modern and scientific, in line with the march of time and progress, was a tremendous asset.

If we're looking for a specific entry point into Virginia during the time of Carrie Buck, there are many doorways we might pass through. Most recently, in *Imbeciles: The Supreme Court, American Eugenics, and the Sterilization of Carrie Buck*, Adam Cohen begins in the Dobbses' "tidy home" on Charlottesville's Grove Street. Paul Lombardo starts in the county circuit court in Amherst, Virginia, where a sham trial was held to move Carrie Buck's fate one step closer to the Supreme Court. Gregory Dorr starts with Thomas Jefferson, founder of the University of Virginia and the state's most beloved son. In *Notes on the State of Virginia*, Jefferson had employed hereditarian thinking to articulate the "natural differences" between races. Musing why a farmer might purposefully breed animals but not society men, he relied on what Dorr calls "the barn-to-bedroom analogy from which all eugenic schemes extended."

Well, if a bedroom is good enough for Thomas Jefferson, let us start in a bedroom.

On September 27, 1916, a poor white woman named Willie Mallory was arrested in a bedroom of her home in the Fulton neighborhood of Richmond, Virginia. In the undoing of the family that took place over the next two years, the Mallorys maintained the arrest had been part of a sting operation. A police officer pretending to want a room to rent had entered their home on false pretenses, the Mallorys alleged, with a plan to arrest Willie for prostitution if she took him near a bedroom.

Instead of prosecuting her, the state ordered Willie be committed to the Virginia State Colony for Epileptics and Feebleminded in Lynchburg, about one hundred miles west of Richmond. Her two teenage daughters, Jessie and Nannie, were also committed to the Colony at the same time. Six months after their arrival, Willie and Jessie underwent operations that left them infertile. The Colony's superintendent, Albert Priddy, claimed the infertility was only a side effect of treatments required to cure them of other reproductive issues. In 1918, the Mallory family sued for damages related to Willie's illegal sterilization and also for the return of their younger children, who had been placed in foster care at the time of Willie's arrest. According to Paul Lombardo and Gregory Dorr, the legal challenges instigated by the Mallorys helped galvanize support among lawmakers and physicians to achieve the passage of a state law permitting eugenic sterilization.

I am telling you about Willie and her daughters because their story introduces the attitudes and the cast of characters that became all too familiar by the time Carrie Buck was sterilized without her consent at the Lynchburg Colony in 1927. But I am also telling you about Willie because I want you to understand what those characters and attitudes looked like when they were not on their best behavior, when they were still working, to some degree, in the shadows.

Carrie Buck's fate was cruel, but in 1927 it was also by the book. In between Willie Mallory's arrest and Carrie Buck's sterilization, Virginia had six years to prepare for scrutiny—to polish its experts, to assemble its best lawyers, and to present arguments that had been decades in the making. Carrie Buck was a passive actor in the legal challenge brought in her name; her legal advocates were simply representatives of the Colony who were playing for the other side to make the case look weak for the benefit of the courts. The Mallory family, on the other hand, caught the state off guard. Albert Priddy was furious for having to justify his actions and answer to allegations made by people he considered degenerate and defective. Willie's legal record is filled with petulance from Priddy and other experts like him. It is thick with their meanness, starting with her initial commitment.

The Lynchburg Colony had opened in 1910 as a home for white epileptic men. Just one year later, Priddy began to reorient the site as an institution central to containing what the state would, again and again, refer to as "the menace of the feebleminded." What was a feebleminded person? There are a number of definitions contemporary to this period, but perhaps the most concise was a person who was "hereditarily deficient in mental capacity." The feebleminded were a catchall group of people—the delinquent, criminal, or promiscuous— that society found unproductive in some way.

I prefer the State of Virginia's definition of "feebleminded," however, used by the State Board of Charities and Corrections as early as 1915: someone who is "permanently and expensively anti-social."

"Permanently" reflects well the dominant mood of the era toward people perceived as troublesome. Borrowing from contemporary theories of crime and punishment, eugenicists saw few cases as correctable. Instead, their methods largely focused on segregating, in some way, the good from the bad. Virginia's definition also helps us understand why people who were classified as "feebleminded" were thought to be so dangerous. The root of their harm—the reason they were holding society back—was that they were "expensive." Someone else was paying for them and that expensive debt would have to be maintained by future generations.

Eugenicists built an intentional glitch in the matrix in their invention of this group: among white people, you couldn't tell if someone was feebleminded simply by looking at them, speaking to them, or watching them work. To the untrained eye, they were indistinguishable from people perceived as "normal." "These people," the state warned, "have none of the stigmata of the lower grade of mental deficients, and are not as easily recognized." The fear of invisible contamination was a potent tool eugenicists used to build power around their set of beliefs, but it also gave them a way to bend reality around the fact that they were, in fact, often targeting people on the basis of presumed character flaws.

Eugenicists used a version of the Simon-Binet Intelligence Test, one adapted by a psychologist named Lewis Terman, to quantify and assess deficient mental capacity when it was needed. Terman was fairly explicit that he had adapted the intelligence scales to ensnare so-called feebleminded people, writing in 1916 that he hoped his work would "ultimately result in curtailing the reproduction of feeblemindedness and in the elimination of an enormous amount of crime, pauperism, and industrial inefficiency." The test results yielded information that helped eugenicists further label people within this group, classifying them as "idiots," "imbeciles," and "morons."

Terman's reference to "industrial inefficiency" is also revealing. Virginia, with its new methods, had painted itself into a corner. To stop white feebleminded individuals from reproducing, it had to contain them somehow. From an economic perspective, simply jailing them was inefficient and wasteful. But the state certainly couldn't solve the problem by confining *fewer* people, which would mean the feebleminded could freely wreak havoc on the society around them.

And so the Lynchburg Colony was born. Its mother was a workhouse, its father an asylum.

Virginia framed its aspirations for the Colony in a special publication titled *Mental Defectives in Virginia*, produced by the State Board of Charites and Correction in 1915, one year before Willie Mallory would arrive at the Lynchburg Colony. The report offers a glowing assessment of a similar institution in Massachusetts, highlighting its efficiency, industry, and order:

> In the laundry we found 70 women at work, 60 of them being 3 to 10 years old mentally. Some of the inmates have become very proficient weavers; last year they wove 4,000 yards of mats and carpets. In the sewing department girls 6 to 10 years old mentally were busily plying their needles and running sewing machines. Last year they turned out 1,200 dresses, 6,000 shirts, and 2,000 stockings. They also spin, knit, and are dextrous at lace-making. Out on the farm we saw 40 low-grade inmates, of 4 to 5 years mental age, clearing up land—digging up stumps and picking off stones; others 6 to 9 years mentally were working with them, doing the plowing and handling of the heavier stumps.

Could Virginia also make its feebleminded population as "economically efficient" as Massachusetts's? Perhaps it could do even better. The same report noted that Virginia prisons made money by selling the labor of incarcerated men. "Every year the penitentiary earns a profit," the state insisted. "They would earn as much in a colony."

The feebleminded, the state reasoned, would always be antisocial. But under the right conditions, they could become less expensive and perhaps even profitable. Two years later, a petition filed by the Mallory family to release Nannie from the Lynchburg Colony would claim that she was being held not for her health, but for her labor. "Nannie Mallory is sane, not feebleminded," the petition read, "and is now in an actual state of involuntary servitude, being now, and ever has been, since her incarceration, a servant or nurse in said Feebleminded Colony without compensation—contrary to the provisions of the United States Constitution."

Before Willie, Jessie, and Nannie were taken to the Lynchburg Colony, the Mallorys looked like any large family—eight children at home, two working parents and two teenage daughters earning wages, and an older woman, a family friend, sharing expenses as a lodger. By choice or necessity, Willie's husband George worked outside of Richmond sawing timber but traveled home on weekends. They struggled with money and finding stability, but they also marshalled a number of character witnesses at their trial who testified the Mallorys were an otherwise respectable family.

The Mallorys were relatively recent transplants, and prior to life in Richmond they had lived in a rural community on the city's outskirts. Moving to the city brought them into contact with the system. George drank too much once and received a warning from the law. Willie lost a child during a difficult birth and her hospital stay was extended due to distress. Not long before Willie's arrest in 1916, the family's house caught fire and they collected a small sum from a private charity to pay one month's rent on a new home. George thought he had cleared the debt; he later testified he went to chop wood for the man who ran the charity and considered that an even exchange. But perhaps the encounter with charity was the key that opened the door to the terrible world they would be forced into; the Mallorys accepted money, which means they became a burden.

The state looked at a family like the Mallorys and saw a chaotic, burdensome unit that could be split into more productive individual parts. And that's what it did. Six minor children were placed in foster care and three women were institutionalized indefinitely at a place where they could not get pregnant, but they could work.

The day after Willie's arrest, a woman named Sarah Roller, who worked for Richmond's courts, told Willie she'd be taken that afternoon for a brief visit with her children. Willie was overjoyed, she later explained, and fixed her appearance as best she could to try to conceal the fact that she was wearing a jail apron. But the true purpose of the outing was to have Willie assessed for admission to the Lynchburg Colony.

Willie, still thinking about her children, was compliant with the process. And yet, something about the way the assessment unfolded seemed off to her. She later described Roller supervising the process as two physicians asked "all sorts of foolish questions." "A doctor examined my mind," Willie stated in one of the Mallory depositions, "and asked if I could tell whether salt was in bread, and did I know how to tie my shoes. There was a picture hanging on the wall of a dog. He asked me if it was a dog or a lady."

Willie believed she performed well and that this

disappointed Roller.

"I can't get that woman in," Willie recalled the examiner telling Roller. Then, according to Willie, Roller responded, "Put on there, 'unable to control her nerves,' and we can get her in for that."

The year before Willie, Jessie, and Nannie Mallory arrived at the Lynchburg Colony, the Virginia Board of Charities and Corrections had recommended that the state "prevent by segregation or sterilization the procreation of the feebleminded." The Board added that "only by striking at the fountainhead . . . can we hope to dry up the springs of this evil." For those who advocated for sterilization, however, the problem was that it was not strictly legal in Virginia.

Indiana had passed a eugenic sterilization law in 1907, the first of its kind in the United States. Indiana also happened to be home to a prison physician named Harry Sharp, who had perfected a technique for administering vasectomies on the job. "I do it without administering an anesthetic either general or local," he wrote in the *Journal of the American Medical Association*. "It requires about three minutes' time to perform the operation and the subject returns to his work immediately." But eugenic sterilization, inspired by Sharp and enshrined in Indiana law "to prevent procreation of confirmed criminals, idiots, imbeciles and rapists," was suspended in 1909 by Thomas R. Marshall, a new governor who believed the law was on shaky constitutional footing.

Virginia had its own version of Harry Sharp. In 1910, Richmond prison surgeon Charles Carrington revealed, in the *Virginia Medical Semi-Monthly*, that he had, for some years, subjected incarcerated men to castration and, later, to vasectomy. His boasts included the story of how he had transformed a "debased little negro" into a "sleek, fat, docile" fellow, almost pet-like, through sterilization.

Carrington, quite rightly as it happened, predicted that his methods, if they were put to a legal test, would be regarded as cruel and unusual, and Virginia failed in its first attempt around this time to build support for a law similar to Indiana's. But Carrington urged solidarity among physicians in the South to achieve the passage of sterilization laws aimed at habitual criminals and, in a nod to eugenic thought, unfit families. In his essay, "Sterilization of Habitual Criminals," he wrote:

> I have been a surgeon to the penitentiary for over ten years, a long enough time to see father and then sons come to the prison, and by looking back over records, I learned that the grandfather had also been an inmate. Now this hideous reproduction of criminals, from father to son to grandson, should be stopped; it is right and proper that it should be, and it will be in time—in a very short time, too—if you doctors of Virginia will awaken to the importance of this proposition as a crime preventer, and tell your Representatives in the House and Senate that from a medical and surgical standpoint it is a good measure.

Virginia's first eugenic experiments clearly targeted men who were thought to be habitually criminal or deviant and who, in Carrington's sample, were disproportionately Black. So how did it happen that, barely five years after Carrington was writing about incarcerated men, poor white women like Willie Mallory became the public face of the state's eugenic anxieties?

Think of eugenics not as a science, but as a solution to a collective fear; that someday, a world might exist where wealth and whiteness did not guarantee power. The destabilization to what many eugenicists considered the "natural order" might arrive on two fronts: from Black and other nonwhite people securing rights, privileges, and access to space, a process eugenicists felt would be hastened along by interracial marriage and procreation, and from worthless white people, especially women, contaminating the race from within by producing defective children.

When elite, white Virginians expressed horror at a lurking, feebleminded menace, they were most often thinking of other white people and particularly white women. These Virginians already regarded all Black people as eugenically compromised, possessing able-bodies but weak minds, and skin color provided the tell. Achieving greater social control over white women, they reasoned, could help prevent the production of biracial children who would impair their ability to "see" race and arrange their society accordingly.

Virginia, like all Southern states, had methods in place—racial segregation, disenfranchisement, incarceration, extralegal violence—to achieve social control over Black people. What it didn't have was a reliable method to efficiently control the large population of what it considered "unfit" white people. So Virginia built toward two goals—twin defenses on the same battlefield. The first was a Racial Integrity Act designed to reinforce segregation and affix a standard of racial purity for white people. The second was a compulsory sterilization law. It achieved both in 1924.

Virginia still institutionalized, and later sterilized, so-called feebleminded Black people and those with other perceived disabilities at Central State Hospital in Petersburg, around thirty miles south of Richmond. Much like attitudes toward white patients, the physicians at Central State believed that what they labeled insanity or mental weakness in Black patients was a sign of "race degeneration." But specific to Black patients, these physicians also believed that an abundance of freedom could trigger insanity or mental decline. Eugenics allowed conventional and stereotypical beliefs about Black people to become medicialized, while at the same time transferring many of these beliefs onto white subjects as a new form of disability.

Despite the persistence of prison surgeons, the sterilization of incarcerated men had not helped their crusade in the eyes of the wider world. It made eugenic sterilization seem like a punishment, when it needed to look like a unique, modern intervention that had universal benefits for society, including, as a bonus, for the unfit. In this quest, women's anatomy and social position were more helpful tools. Medicine had rooted all manner of disease and weakness in their reproductive system in the past. If an immoral lifestyle existed in a patient, the thinking went, it would leave its evidence there. Operations were to be expected.

At the Lynchburg Colony, just before the Mallory women arrived, Albert Priddy had taken to literally operating outside of the law. Paul Lombardo has noted that under Priddy's supervision, there was "an amazingly coincidental pattern of sterilization among women judged to be 'morons' who also had the ill fortune of suffering from 'pelvic diseases' of vague and unspecified etiology." Priddy wanted to sterilize even more women, not only because he thought it a eugenically sound decision, but because he believed sterilized women were more efficient, productive workers. In his view, the women who had been coincidentally sterilized at the Colony had "gone out into the world and [were] earning their own good living under the care of proper persons, and behaving themselves well."

Willie and Jessie Mallory became part of these statistics. Because Jessie had been sterilized, she was released from the Colony shortly after her operation and placed as a maid with a family one hundred miles from her own to test her abilities to work and behave under what Priddy called "the care of proper persons." The conditions imposed on Willie after her release were cruel in a different way. Not only was she the cause of all of this trouble through what Priddy saw as her hyperactive fertility, but she was also a difficult and uncompliant patient with at least one escape attempt. Under threat of recommitment, Priddy forbade Willie from ever reuniting with her younger children or her husband, even though she could no longer get pregnant. Her eldest daughter Irene, who lived with her husband outside of Richmond, took her in. Nannie's fate was yet to be determined. Having proven herself as a source of valuable labor at the Lynchburg Colony by caring for some of its younger wards, she remained committed there.

In order to reunite, the Mallorys had to do something unthinkable for a poor family that the state now viewed as deeply antisocial: they had to take Albert Priddy and the State of Virginia to court. Their legal challenges became the basis for three separate actions: a petition to free Nannie from the Lynchburg Colony, a petition to secure the return of their young children, and a suit for damages against Priddy for illegal sterilization. "There is no law for such treatment," George Mallory had warned Priddy in a letter, referring to Willie's questionable operation, "I am a poor man but smart anuf to find that out."

Today, Albert Priddy isn't notable enough to even claim his own Wikipedia entry, but in 1917 he arranged himself with all the confidence of a man who believed his actions would not only see vindication by the court but by all generations that came after him. Answering to a poor family was a blow to his ego, which he attempted to soothe by menacing the Mallorys even as a legal dispute seemed all but assured. Priddy threatened to have the entire family committed. He told George he had the power to have him arrested. He wrote letters to the Mallorys claiming that Willie and Jessie had begged for their operations, and he insisted the women owed him thanks for helping them overcome their "life of shame."

Behind this vicious bluster, however, Priddy was slightly panicked. Neither he nor Sarah Roller had double-checked the commitment paperwork for the Mallory women, perhaps because they were working in collusion or perhaps because procedures had recently changed and both of them failed to notice the paperwork was incomplete. This mistake helped the Mallory family win the return of their children, including Nannie, in early 1918. But it was insufficient to secure any damages for the illegal operations. The court agreed with Priddy that "the defendant, a practicing physician, was honestly of the opinion that the plaintiff would be materially benefitted by a surgical operation."

Broadly, the Mallory case helped unify the superintendents of Virginia's other state institutions; they were afraid of their own day in court and more eager than ever to secure a law that explicitly legalized eugenic sterilization. No one wanted to be humiliated like Priddy, forced to downplay their work as something that was only beneficial to worthless women. There was a better world to build, and it would not be done in the shadows.

But for the Mallory family, shadows likely became an important tool for their continued survival after their reunion. Historian Steven Noll, who looked at the Mallory case in the context of broader legal attitudes toward poor mothers, believes the family left Richmond soon after the verdicts. There is no evidence of them in city directories after 1918. It's possible that the Mallorys believed Priddy and his surrogates intended to make good on their menacing promises to break up the family again. Noll, like me, places odds on the family reverting to "their previous anonymous status as a poor working family trying simply to survive."

In the years following the Mallory lawsuit, Priddy became an expert lobbyist. He had a strong ally in the Virginia General Assembly named Aubrey Strode, a lawyer turned state senator who had been instrumental in the creation of the Lynchburg Colony. In 1919, soon after the Mallory case had concluded, Strode set to work writing a number of bills that lent additional legal protections to hospital superintendents and made it more difficult for patients to challenge their commitments. These laws were welcome contributions, but they were not the ultimate prize.

In 1921, Virginia elected a new governor, E. Lee Trinkle, who was sympathetic to eugenics and also desperate to reduce the state's budget. Trinkle's administration indicated it would be receptive to a sterilization law as a way to cull the populations of state institutions and cut costs. Institutionalization, like incarceration, lent itself to flexible arguments. It could be expensive when the state needed to paint the confined population as a financial burden. But if a desire arose to expand the system, to lock up more people, then the system could be framed as remarkably efficient, a machine that economically sustained itself through institutional labor.

According to Paul Lombardo, for example, the costs associated with confinement at state hospitals at this particular time were actually decreasing. What was increasing were the costs associated with modernizing a state, like building new roads and other infrastructure. Following a long tradition, with some old-fashioned sleight of hand, Virginia's poor and vulnerable people became a useful example of the kind of obstacles that were limiting the state's potential.

The complications and legal challenges faced by states trying to enact eugenic sterilization laws concerned the leaders of the Eugenic Record Office, the control center of the national movement based in New York. California had a broad law on the books since 1909, but in other states, the legislative process had either stalled or been unsuccessful. But the Eugenics Record Office employed Harry Laughlin, a Princeton-trained biologist whose passion project, when he wasn't doling out nativist, anti-immigration polemics for Congress, was tracking the successes and failures of compulsory sterilization laws nationwide. In 1922, he perfected a model law that would soon be of great use to Audrey Strode.

Closer to home, but also working in sympathy with the national crusade, the University of Virginia in Charlottesville was blazing its own path to usefulness for the eugenics movement. The university had heady ambitions, none of which was more important than showing the world that the South was still a force to be reckoned with, a place more than capable of producing great men.

Gregory Michael Dorr, whose book *Segregation's Science* charts the importance of the University of Virginia to the wider national eugenics movement, writes, "The scientific stance" embedded in eugenic philosophies "allowed elite Virginians to claim that they represented the vanguard of modern social engineering, ushering in a future that looked suspiciously like the past."

Eugenics allowed the plantation owner to speak with the mouth of a scientist; it eased the transition between the old and the new. And the University of Virginia, through its influence and its faculty, did the same by proselytizing eugenic truths. The great men predicted by university president Edwin Alderman, and trained by the eugenicists he elevated up the faculty ranks, would not be generals, but he saw them fighting a battle for the future just the same.

For Alderman and many of the faculty appointed during his tenure, building a modern, progressive university on the foundations of white supremacy was not a paradoxical endeavor. In Virginia, eugenics became an important tool to reclaim Southern identity; not a backward or self-conscious one—surely the South's reputation had suffered enough for its crimes—but an enlightened one. Dorr calls this strategy Virginia's "middle passage," a way for the state and its esteemed institutions to be both Northern (enlightened) and Southern (traditional) at the same time. Paul Brandon Barringer, Alderman's predecessor and the architect of the university's medical program, had previously set a similar tone. Barringer's reputation as a scientific thinker advanced steadily after he took "the Negro problem" as his subject and marked it with his version of hereditarian insight. "His late tendency to return to barbarism," Barringer wrote, referring to modern Black people, "is as natural as the return of a sow that is washed to her wallowing in the mire."

Barringer's book, *The American Negro: His Past and Future*, continues: "Fortunately for us, experience (history) also shows that these savage traits can be held down, and we have seen that if held down long enough, they will be bred out. In this fact lies the hope of the South." You're reading that right—Barringer was suggesting that slavery was a beneficial institution to both the enslaved and society at large. It's an old argument, of course, but one that Barringer freshened up and modernized through the emergence of eugenics and race science.

The University of Virginia championed education and science as the cornerstones of a new South. In the early twentieth century, it set to work producing discoveries that affirmed white racial superiority and provided leverage that was useful to bend the future toward its truths. Its most important leverage was its alumni, and by the 1920s, UVA could claim two decades' worth of leaders who populated the ranks of the medical profession, public health agencies, and appointed and elected offices throughout the state. They had been molded by a curriculum that scientifically condemned Black people and viewed unfit whites as the enemy within.

Aubrey Strode was a graduate of the University of Virginia's law program. He was also, curiously, the son of two parents who died institutionalized. This meant he was in worse shape, eugenically speaking, than Carrie Buck, the young woman whose misfortunes would soon make his career. But no matter. When the rich failed to reach perfection, hereditary concerns could easily be taken off the table by a friendly physician. In Strode's case, the family doctor assured him (quite rightly) that no one should be concerned by the "mental aberration" of his parents and that he should move forward with his life without stigma.

Using the model law Harry Laughlin had developed and prepared under the auspices of the Eugenics Record Office, Strode devised a bill for Virginia's 1924 legislative session that would permit the sterilization of "defective persons . . . likely to become by propagation of their kind a menace to society." The law's language was broad, but other provisions were added to assure Virginia's well-to-do families (like Strode's) with embarrassing skeletons in their closets that no one would be coming for *their kind*. There was a structured appeals process, for example, that might tax a court-appointed guardian who was representing dozens of indigent patients, but wouldn't affect the well-connected who had attorneys and friendly physicians at their disposal. Only two votes in the entire House and Senate combined dissented against the bill. On March 20, 1924, E. Lee Trinkle signed it into law.

These were the networks of power that were assembling at the same time Carrie Buck, a quiet orphaned teenager, was keeping house in Charlottesville for John and Alice Dobbs.

The Buck family resembled the Mallorys in many ways, by which I mean they were an unsympathetically poor white family and unable to remain anonymous due to tragic circumstances. Also like the Mallorys, Carrie's parents, Emma and Frank, were likely part of a larger demographic shift at the turn of the century that saw rural people moving closer to cities to take part in new, industrialized employment.

Emma and Frank's 1896 marriage certificate indicates they both were from Albemarle County and intended to reside in the county seat of Charlottesville. It also indicates that there was an almost twenty-year age difference between Frank and Emma; she was twenty-three, he was forty-two.

Carrie, their first child, was born ten years later in 1906. It is not easy to know what Frank and Emma's first decade of marriage looked like because they had not yet captured the state's interest. Adam Cohen, the author of *Imbeciles: The Supreme Court, American Eugenics, and the Sterilization of Carrie Buck*, suggests that Frank worked as a tinsmith, an occupation soon to be doomed by the mass production of low-cost metal in Northern factories. He was fifty-two when Carrie was born, and soon after, catastrophe hit. We don't know what happened exactly. Frank died, or it's possible he cut his losses and abandoned his family. Emma began referring to herself as a widow, although historians speculate whether this was actually true.

Welfare and social assistance as we think of it today did not exist in Emma Buck's world. For a woman like her, raising a child on her own, survival often meant relying on aid provided by private and religious charities. Moral improvement, however, was an expected condition of remaining on the "charity list." Emma tried but failed in this, in the eyes of charity workers, by becoming a mother to a second daughter and a son in her early, questionable widowhood. Harry Laughlin, as an expert witness in *Buck v. Bell*, would later fabricate a history for Emma that included a divorce based on her infidelity, which made her "maritally unworthy," and a descent into prostitution.

Whatever the reality, Emma, as a poor mother with children who were presumed to be illegitimate, was easily labeled a deviant. And in this era, sexual deviancy was a sign of a deeper mental degeneracy. "They are people whom the community has tolerated and helped to support, at the same time that it has deplored their vices and their inefficiency," wrote influential eugenicist Henry Goddard in 1912. He argued that people who fit that description, like Emma, belonged to a previously undetectable class of genetically defective people who needed to be managed through segregation and perhaps even sterilization.

The courts first intervened in Emma's life when they removed Carrie from her care and placed her with foster parents, John and Alice Dobbs, around 1910, when Carrie was three or four years old. Emma's circumstances only worsened, however. She remained trapped in poverty, and the state presumed that, as a woman often experiencing homelessness, she was likely engaging in prostitution. The state committed her to the Lynchburg Colony in 1920. There, staff used intelligence testing to label her a "moron," a class of people who were typically confined for life.

At the time of her mother's commitment, Carrie was fourteen years old and still living with the Dobbs family on Grove Street. Unlike the Dobbses' slightly older biological daughter, Carrie had stopped attending school after she completed the fifth grade. By most metrics, her scholastic performance was average and in some subjects quite good, but the Dobbses ended her education to free her up to serve as the family housekeeper. Adam Cohen suggests that the Dobbses hired Carrie out as a maid to other neighborhood families as well.

In 1923, Carrie, then seventeen years old, became pregnant. Alice's nephew, Clarence Garland, raped her while the Dobbses were out of town. Carrie, it seems, had visions of Clarence claiming the child, somehow making some part of this right by her, but he fled Charlottesville, and no one who could find him cared to. It is clear, from what soon unfolded, that the Dobbses preferred to think of their nephew as an innocent party who acted unwisely after crossing paths with an immoral woman. But even this less disturbing version of events implied that John and Alice had failed to guide Carrie toward moral improvement, which was part of their responsibility as foster parents. The potential for scandal was enormous.

The Dobbses eventually set in motion a plan to have Carrie, who had lived with the family for more than a decade, committed to the same institution where her mother lived. In January 1924, they filed a legal petition declaring that Carrie was both epileptic *and* feebleminded, conditions that were not mutually exclusive but certainly not comorbid in the way that John and Alice, trying hard to stack the deck, seemed to hope. A most important condition, however, went unmentioned in the petition: Carrie's pregnancy. On one hand, her pregnancy could have been proof of her defective character; on the other, it might have invited questions about paternity. Perhaps its omission had something to do with the fact that the Colony didn't accept pregnant women.

The Dobbses wrote that they had taken Carrie in "as an act of kindness," but, due to a decline in her behavior, they could no longer "care for said girl financially, or be responsible for her safe control." As a final act of kindness, I am sure, the Dobbses also manufactured for Carrie an incoherent history of disturbing behavior, violent outbursts, and hallucinations that had allegedly been ongoing, though they had never been previously reported. With all bases sufficiently covered, Carrie was committed to the Lynchburg Colony by the same judge who had ordered her mother's confinement just four years earlier.

By this time, Carrie was eighteen and around seven months pregnant. She was also now technically under custody of the Lynchburg Colony, which eventually deferred her admission until after the baby was born. This meant Carrie was also homeless. John and Alice refused to let Carrie remain in their home, perhaps because their biological daughter, who lived at the home with her husband, was also expecting a child at the same time. Carrie gave birth to her daughter, Vivian, in March 1924 in a temporary placement arranged by social workers.

The Dobbses agreed to accept custody of Vivian, but why they did is a painful, somewhat unanswerable question. Did they keep her because she was their niece and they felt some compassion for the child? Or was it because social workers guilted them into doing it, explaining that infants could not be institutionalized until they were around eight years old and that it would be difficult to place Vivian with a different family? We will never know what plans the Dobbses ultimately intended for Vivian's life; she died from colitis when she was eight.

In what is possibly Carrie Buck's only recorded interview, which she gave to a reporter from National Public Radio's *Horizons* program in 1980, she described this entire arc of her life with two clipped sentences.

"I had a baby and I had to leave Charlottesville. This here guy, he took advantage of me, that was all."

Ask me what is easier to find than the sound of Carrie Buck's voice and I will tell you it is *the testimony of the men who condemned her.* In the official legal record that spanned years on its journey to the United States Supreme Court, Carrie speaks only once, responding to a question from Aubrey

Strode, the author of Virginia's sterilization law and, in these legal proceedings, the Lynchburg Colony's attorney:

> Q: "Do you care to say anything about having this operation performed on you?"
> A: "No sir, I have not, it's up to my people."

The first time you read this, you might assume, especially if you are Southern like me, that by "my people," Carrie meant her family. But that wasn't her meaning because she no longer had a family. Her people now were her lawyers and legal advocates. And they were another group who would, with incalculable cruelty, work against her interests in service of the state's larger ambitions.

Securing a sterilization law in Virginia had been a significant victory for its advocates, but before the law went into practice, its architects felt it would need a strong legal test. A first patient would be selected and supplied with counsel, who would then execute the appeals process all the way from the hospital board to the highest court in the country. Carrie Buck was the perfect first subject. Her childbearing years stretched out before her, she had given birth to a questionable child already, and her own mother had also been institutionalized.

Staff at the Lynchburg Colony assessed Carrie as being physically healthy but "feeble-minded of the lowest grade, moron class." By July 1924, in accordance with the new law, Albert Priddy had prepared the documents required to seek her sterilization. The Lynchburg Colony's board held a perfunctory hearing at their September meeting and granted permission for the operation.

The board agreed to find Carrie an attorney to appeal the decision, and to appoint one of its own to represent the Colony's interests. Aubrey Strode, who was friends with Priddy, agreed to act as the Colony's attorney during the appeal. Irving Whitehead, another friend and a former Lynchburg Colony board member, was hired to represent Carrie. All of these men were advocates of eugenic sterilization. Carrie's case was not meant to be a true appeal, but more a legally binding theatrical performance.

Today, if you obtain a copy of the filings associated with *Buck v. Bell*, you will also receive a transcript of the first appeal in the circuit court of Amherst County, Virginia, which occurred in November 1924. The case has a different name because Albert Priddy, who spent the final months of his life fighting for the privilege of sterilizing a teenage rape victim, died before the case reached the Supreme Court. The case was passed to his successor, John Bell.

I imagine that Strode was pleased with himself and the weight of expertise he was able to assemble on such short notice. Harry Laughlin of the Eugenics Record Office submitted an interrogatory from New York but sent a top fieldworker, Arthur Estabrook, to appear in court. Joseph DeJarnette represented, along with Albert Priddy, the superintendents of Virginia's state hospitals.

The transcript of the Amherst appeal reads like a dress rehearsal where not everyone knows their lines. DeJarnette admits that he can't really explain Mendel's Laws very well, and butchers them trying to talk about them anyway. Whitehead struggles to ask relevant questions, both because he is not used to thinking of eugenics as something that needs to be justified, but also because he's asking intentionally bad questions to weaken Carrie's defense. Estabrook and Laughlin oversell their case. But none of this matters. It is a foregone conclusion that Carrie will be sterilized.

Whitehead's line of defense went like this: if Virginia were to sterilize feebleminded women, wouldn't those women use their infertility as an excuse to go "on a rampage" and fuck the country into a new crisis of venereal disease? *Seems logical to me*, Whitehead suggests with an implied wink, *that locking these women up for life would be better*. What would ever be worth the risk of such an outcome?

There was, of course, the freedom and happiness of the women to consider; a sterilized life outside an institution was better than a life within the experts insisted, their minds intentionally narrowed to only those two possibilities. But, as DeJarnette explains, "It benefits society by not taking care of them, and by the work they do. They are the hewers of wood and drawers of water." In the Book of Joshua, the "hewers of wood and drawers of water" are the servants of servants, those performing the lowest forms of labor. In other words, DeJarnette was making an argument for sterilization not just as population management, but as a form of employment insurance.

What DeJarnette conveyed with a Biblical flourish, Albert Priddy explained in plainer English:

> The demand for domestics in housework is so great that probably we could get rid of half our young women of average intelligence, but I have had to abolish it. They go out, and it is so common for them to come back pregnant that I have quit taking the risk. People don't care to take them when there is a constant chance of them becoming mothers.

Laughlin, on paper from New York, pronounced the Buck family were part of the "shiftless, ignorant, and worthless class of anti-social whites of the South." Estabrook received a generous fee from the state for offering a similar opinion in person. (Through Paul Lombardo's research, we can also know an infuriating coda to this story: that it was so common for Estabrook to cheat on his wife during his trips that she eventually complained to his superiors, who terminated him around 1929 after discovering he'd inflated his travel expenses to pocket the difference.)

There was no suggestion, no mention, that Carrie had been a victim of rape. She was just a body that was useful once, then was not, but now might be useful again.

Eugenics ended up winning that round in Amherst County. It won again and again, at last in the Supreme Court in 1927. Carrie Buck was sterilized at the Lynchburg Colony on October 19 of that year.

Buck v. Bell made eugenic sterilization legal nationwide. States that wanted to enact their own laws were now free to do so and put them in motion immediately. There was no longer a need to be conservative. By 1963, around 60,000 people in the United States had been sterilized. The record for the highest number of sterilizations procedures performed by a state belongs to California, with at least 20,000 operations performed. New research on recently discovered public health records undertaken by a team led by historian Alexandra Minna Stern has concluded that California's eugenics program disproportionately targeted Latino people, especially women.

When I hear people today describe the men involved in Carrie's case as individuals with flawed but humanitarian motives, I think of Albert Priddy's ridiculous testimony, the audacity with which he complained about a kink in his supply chain. I remember how he grumbled that his institution for feebleminded patients had a surplus of intelligent women, how he testified that, as a superintendent, he was powerless to address that dilemma in the most obvious way, by simply releasing the women unharmed. I think of how low our standards must be if creating better housekeepers by sterilizing poor women counts as a humanitarian action. And then I wonder how many good families in Virginia wanted a Colony girl who was insured for that type of work by being permanently infertile.

Men have raped women workers ever since they were allowed to own them. Everyone in that Amherst County courtroom knew that fact and understood what could happen, what *was* happening, when vulnerable women entered homes far from their own and were expected to be compliant under threat of recommitment. Maybe we have tried so hard to give men like Albert Priddy and Joseph DeJarnette enlightened ideas that we have actually neglected to grant them with common sense. *They go out, and it is so common for them to come back pregnant I have quit taking the risk.* But this is what eugenics in Virginia actually looked like, even out of the shadows; a pathetic guild of men complaining that the very system they controlled was making their lives difficult.

If you try to find the home that Carrie Buck once shared with John and Alice Dobbs in Charlottesville, your excursion will likely end in a parking lot for offices associated with the University of Virginia Health Systems. When I took a field trip there with my partner Josh in September 2019, the organization was in crisis mode after the *Washington Post* had reported on its aggressive debt collection practices. I stood in the parking lot thinking about Carrie, but also about the 36,000 people the University of Virginia had sued in the previous six years to collect on medical bills. I remembered how the school's medical program had flourished under eugenicists, and I wondered if anyone in its modern-day iteration would be brave enough to say that putting healthcare beyond the reach of the poor was just eugenics by a different name.

The University of Virginia began acquiring land in that part of the city in 1965. Most recently, in 2016, it had paid almost $9 million for seven properties on King Street and the nearby

Grove Street, where Carrie lived until she was committed. There are historic photographs of this neighborhood, but my most recent impression of it with the Dobbs home intact is from a news story that aired around 1992. The home was derelict by that point, shockingly close to railroad tracks. Once the periphery of Charlottesville, the neighborhood today is typical of what new residents and investors call revitalization and what many longtime residents call gentrification. In 2008, *C-VILLE Weekly* called the neighborhood, which is only a ten-minute walk from the University of Virginia, a community with "some of the city's least expensive housing in one of the most desirable locations in town."

Since the Dobbses' time, the neighborhood had become predominately Black, but an influx of home flippers and white young professionals who were attached to the University of Virginia were changing that. In 2008 and 2009, when parts of the neighborhood also became a historic district at the insistence of the city's preservation planner, property assessments shot up by 18 percent. Commenting in 2009 on his own decision to purchase investment property in the neighborhood, former Charlottesville Mayor Blake Caravati mused, "I try not to contribute to gentrification, but in fact I do it for a living. I buy old houses and I fix them up." Caravati admitted he knew "hardworking people" who had been "forced to move" because of competition from investors and their impact on property assessments, but the lesson he chose to draw from that loss was "that's just what cities are about in a way."

In *Dispatches from Dystopia*, historian Kate Brown writes, "to describe the places I visit is to admit the partialness and paltriness of knowledge I distill from them." Carrie Buck's former neighborhood doesn't tell us anything about what happened to her after she was sterilized and released from the Lynchburg Colony in 1927. It doesn't tell us in what ways, exactly, the University of Virginia grew as a result of the reputation it earned in part from its larder of eugenicists. But it does tell us that enormous growth did occur and helped create changes across the entire city that the early twentieth-century version of Charlottesville would find pleasing. The replacement of poor white people and all Black people with better, white citizens was an outcome its past version would admire.

I knew I wouldn't be able to find evidence of Carrie's home when I went looking for it. But that was the point. I knew, but also wanted to *feel*, what comes next in this story: a great absence and paltriness of meaning.

Up until 1944, we can still find Carrie in archival records because she continued to correspond with the Lynchburg Colony about her mother. In Adam Cohen's *Imbeciles*, he notices the exact same thing I did about this correspondence—no one from the Colony wrote to Carrie as if she were feebleminded. But once Emma died, that correspondence ends. After that, the parts of Carrie we are allowed to know become fragments.

When Carrie was paroled from the Lynchburg Colony just weeks after her surgery, she was sent to work as a housekeeper for the owners of a lumber operation near Radford, around a hundred miles away. The placement did not take. Carrie used one of the home's better pieces of crockery as a chamber pot and was returned to the Colony. In 1928, the Newberry family in Seddon, three hours away, wrote to superintendent John Bell, who had become the Colony's new superintendent after Albert Priddy's death, that they were "really anxious to get a good girl from your institution." That good girl became Carrie, introduced through correspondence from Bell to the Newberrys as "strong and healthy and capable of doing good work." Similar to her first placement, the Newberrys would be required to pay the cost of Carrie's transportation to Seddon and give her wages of $5 a month (around $75 in today's money). Bell confirmed receipt of the Newberrys' advance payment for Carrie's transportation and reassured them, "She is 22 years of age, strong and healthy, and should render good services." If their arrangement with Carrie ceased to be beneficial to them, the Newberrys could send her back to the Colony.

The Newberrys thought they were on the road to doing exactly that shortly after Carrie's arrival. In December 1928, they wrote to Bell that Carrie, "an old hand at the business," was "beginning her adultery again." Carrie knew a bad report was coming and attempted to write to Bell personally to explain: "Dr. Bell I am expecting Mrs. Newberry to write you about some trouble I have had but I hope you will not put it against me and have me come back there as I am trying now to make a good record and get my discharge." Carrie, incidentally, had perfect penmanship. But contrary to the Newberrys' first expectations, Carrie remained with them for an additional four years. The Newberrys gave her no more unfavorable reports, although they did urge Bell to "keep a good girl in reserve" for them just in case.

In 1928, Carrie wrote another letter to the Lynchburg Colony that, although short, is filled with meaning. She addressed it to a hospital worker she calls Mrs. Coleman, and the letter asks if there is any news about her half sister, who was also now institutionalized. She writes, "I guess there are a lot of girls going away now." More sterilized women were making their way out into the world and workforce. Carrie explains that she is tardy in responding to her mother's latest letter but can't take the time to respond at that moment "as I have got some work to do." It concludes with a request for permission to send her mother some things, which she does not specify. All of that control in a letter that is not even one hundred words long.

In 1932, Carrie married William Eagle, a sixty-three-year-old widower. She was twenty-six. She wrote to Bell just a few days after her marriage, letting him know, "I thought it best for me to marry." Carrie and William lived modestly. She loved working in her garden and tried to make plans for her mother to come and live with them, but by then Emma was too fragile to be put through a long move. William died in 1941. Carrie finally saved the money to visit her mother in 1944, but when she arrived, staff told her that Emma had died the previous spring.

What happened to Carrie after William Eagle's death is less clear. At some point she moved to Front Royal, Virginia, a small community near Winchester, about four hours from Seddon. It seems likely that she reunited with her siblings and this opened up more possibilities for her. In 1965, she married Charlie Detamore. Carrie and Charlie, both in their sixties, sometimes worked as apple pickers in Front Royal, but Carrie more often did domestic work and acted as a caregiver. They decided to move to Charlottesville around 1970. Like Carrie, Charlie was from Charlottesville originally, and so, perhaps understanding they were close to the end of their lives, they decided to go home.

If you try to find evidence about Carrie's married life, you might, like me, attempt this first from the comfort of home by searching online census records. This strategy produces many results from genealogical websites. These genealogists are often more frank about the circumstances of Carrie's life than textbooks tend to be. They use words like "forced," "coerced," and, "involuntary." Some, perhaps aware of Paul Lombardo's work, proudly note Carrie's daughter Vivian was an honor student. Many people claim to be her distant relatives. Dozens have left virtual flowers for her through the websites that list the location of her grave. It's the people who are interested in inheritance who now most emphatically claim her.

———

Even at the Colony, which by the time of Carrie's move back to Charlottesville was called the Lynchburg Training School, they did not claim her. Dr. K. Ray Nelson, who was the director there in the 1970s, hadn't even known about the institution's past before he took the position. He eventually caught up, and he wondered what had happened to Carrie. Then one day, in 1979, he received a request from a former patient who was struggling to complete an application for Social Security. A birth certificate could not be located, and a medical record would be needed to confirm her eligibility.

This request eventually led Nelson to a home in Front Royal that belonged to Doris Figgins. She was about to learn two important facts about herself: she was sixty-seven years old, and when she was sixteen she had been sterilized without her consent. He wasn't prepared for her reaction to the news. "I can't tell you the empathy I felt for her when I realized she had not been told she'd been sterilized," Nelson told Charlottesville's *Daily Progress* in 1980. "Here was this lady who for years had been feeling that she failed because couldn't have children. It wasn't her fault at all." Doris was also Carrie Buck's younger sister. Nelson took the story to the press with the blessing of Doris and her husband, Matthew. "I never knew what was done to me," headlines repeated in the voice of Doris's grief.

The following year, the ACLU sued Virginia on behalf of a group of anonymous patients who had been sterilized at state institutions. The lawsuit hoped to have the forced surgeries declared unconstitutional. A few years earlier, in 1974, Virginia had repealed, somewhat quietly, the state's Sterilization Act. In 1979, it had removed a similar provision in the law for the sterilization of those with "hereditary forms of mental illness that are recurrent." But the precedent set by *Buck v. Bell* remained, as it does to this day.

A few reporters were able to track Carrie down through

Doris and Nelson. Most reporters who crossed paths with Carrie and Charlie at that time described their home as a shed or shack that lacked both plumbing and electricity, and that the couple was badly malnourished and living in dire poverty. Charlie was bedridden. I do not know, but I imagine that Carrie, by that point, had drawn the same lesson from her life that I have—that for the poor, anonymity can be a safer option than seeking help that might not ever materialize.

Carrie was unconnected to the ACLU's lawsuit, but she granted brief interviews to Nelson and a few reporters. She allowed Nelson to take her back to Lynchburg to visit her mother's grave. Social workers, much kinder than the versions Carrie encountered in 1924, were able to place her and Charlie in a state nursing facility in nearby Waynesboro. The couple was happy there. Over a span of eighty years, the only concession Virginia gave to Carrie Buck was allowing her to die in peace.

As for her legacy, Virginia's defense in the ACLU lawsuit was predictable and unmovable; the Commonwealth's past actions had been sanctioned by the Supreme Court and there was nothing that could be done about it. In 1985, the United States District Court for the Western District of Virginia agreed, stating, "Regardless of whatever philosophical and sociological valuation may be made regarding involuntary sterilization in terms of current mores and social thought, the fact remains that the general practice and procedure under the old Virginia statute were upheld by the highest court in the land in *Buck v. Bell*."

Virginia did agree to set up a temporary hotline to help former state hospital patients access their medical records, perhaps setting in motion their own Doris Figgins moments. But the ACLU's lawsuit became part of a foundation that researchers, reporters, lawyers, and disability rights advocates continued to build upon. In 1993, for example, filmmaker

Stephen Trombley produced *The Lynchburg Story*, a one-hour documentary about involuntary sterilization in Virginia, which included interviews with former patients.

"I felt like I'd never get out. They said they needed me there for work. They said they didn't have enough painters," Jessie Meadows told reporter Mary Carter Bishop, who would one day write *Don't You Ever*, a book detailing her own discovery late in life of her half brother, Ronnie, who had been committed to Western State Hospital. Ronnie was not sterilized in Staunton, but his life reflects an otherwise familiar arc: a struggling family making a secret of a child who had been sent away.

In 2002, the city of Charlottesville finally decided to claim Carrie Buck as one of its own. Attitudes had changed since the eugenics era, but there was also an anniversary looming: the seventy-fifth year of *Buck v. Bell*. Anniversaries are strange things in the world of historical trauma. They're often less like a dignified moment of reflection and more like a supernatural holiday when the dead are allowed to walk freely without harming the living.

Disability rights activists believed the state should use the occasion to apologize for its role in enabling eugenic sterilization. Phil Theisen of the Lynchburg Depressive Disorders Association had been working on a campaign with Keith Kessler, of Virginia's Disabled Action Committee, to urge lawmakers to take up the cause. "This is a skeleton in the closet for Virginia that will continue to be there until it's addressed forthright," Theisen told CBS in 2001. "An apology would be a historic first, and that makes it all the more important."

The CBS story Theisen appeared in also introduced Raymond Hudlow, who assumed the burden of becoming the eugenics movement's perfect victim. Hudlow's abusive father had committed him to the Lynchburg Colony in 1942 after Raymond had unsuccessfully tried to run away.

He was sterilized there when he was sixteen years old. Later, he joined the military and, over the course of a twenty-one-year career, was awarded a Bronze Star, Purple Heart, and Prisoner of War Medal.

Hudlow explained that his teenage years at the Colony were more traumatic than his time as a prisoner of war in Germany. "They treated us just like hogs, like we had no feelings," he told reporters. Hudlow represented what was to many the most chilling arc of Virginia's eugenics program; the confinement and sterilization of not just "normal" people, but those who inverted every conventional understanding of what it meant to be defective. Hudlow was the kind of person, the logic went, the state was refusing to apologize to.

Compared to Hudlow, though, who received separate honors from the state around the time of the *Buck v. Bell* anniversary, what could be said about Carrie Buck other than that she survived? And how could Virginia make that sound redemptive? Blake Caravati, the mayor of Charlottesville at the time, told reporters, "It's important to remember the history of what we used to do to people. Though she was not as capable as the rest of us . . . it didn't stop her from becoming a great citizen. . . . People with mental or physical disabilities can be just as productive as any of us." Caravati, in his idea of redeeming the less capable through productivity, likely did not sense the shadow of eugenics lurking in his praise.

Still, just before the anniversary, the General Assembly approved a "statement of regret" submitted by Mitch Van Yahres, a delegate from Charlottesville. It was softened from an official apology, but it is a fine statement, clear and concise in many important elements. Becoming the first state to take such a step, Virginia admitted that "eugenics laws were used to target virtually any human shortcoming" and used "respectable, 'scientific' veneer to cover the activities of those who held blatantly racist views."

Did this regret inspire any reparative actions? No. At that time, the state concluded that it would simply carry forward the bland duty—expecting the same of its citizens—to reject "any such abhorrent pseudo-scientific movement in the future."

In 2013, North Carolina passed a measure that entitled survivors of eugenic sterilization to a $50,000 payment from the state. North Carolina had sterilized people in numbers similar to Virginia, around 8,000 total, but it had also disproportionately sterilized Black women, particularly in the 1960s, and had allowed welfare workers to petition for sterilization orders directly. This meant that in North Carolina, unlike Virginia, state-ordered sterilization could be forced on people who did not reside in state facilities. By the sixties, around 60 percent of the people who were involuntarily sterilized in North Carolina were young, Black women. Although the number of sterilizations performed in Virginia was declining by the 1950s and 1960s, some lawmakers began to champion eugenic sterilization again, this time with Black people as the implied target, because they understood that new civil rights legislation would weaken their segregated society. This attempted revival ultimately failed in Virginia, but a similar strategy and contributing motivations took root in North Carolina. Because their cases occurred more recently, North Carolina's program contained elements of both racial and reproductive justice.

Unlike North Carolina, Virginia did not explicitly target Black people for sterilization. During the eugenics era, Virginia sterilized 1,880 Black people and 5,239 white people, figures roughly in line with the state's population breakdown. However, among Black people, women represented around 70 percent of operations. More white women were sterilized than white men, but they represented around 55 percent of operations. This does not mean that Virginia had a "less racist" eugenics program than other Southern states, only that Virginia coupled eugenic sterilization with other methods it felt successful in imposing social order on "undesirable people," such as the state's Racial Integrity Act, which was one of the most restrictive in the nation. Dorr explains, "Even though most eugenicists in Virginia cast blacks as a tremendous threat, the menace of feebleminded whites mating with blacks caused greater alarm." Virginia's eugenicists also likely imagined they would be able to curtail reproduction among Black people by incarcerating Black men. Black women were likely sterilized in greater numbers than Black men because eugenicists felt, similar to their attitudes toward white women, that sterilization would improve their productivity and protect their white employers from scandal.

In 2015, with bipartisan support, Virginia passed a measure similar to North Carolina's. It set the compensation limit at $25,000 per person, estimating in the background, in actuarial terms, that most of the victims of eugenic sterilization would be dead since the peak of operations had occurred in the 1930s. The *Washington Post*'s editorial board called the attempt "so paltry that it fails at even symbolically righting the wrong."

"It benefits society by not taking care of them, and by the work they do. They are the hewers of wood and drawers of water," Joseph DeJarnette testified in 1924, describing Carrie Buck's place in the world.

Almost sixty years later, when she was questioned by reporters about what had happened to her, Carrie asked, "I won't get in trouble if I tell, will I?" She did not get in trouble, but at that point in her life, she was very sick. According to Ray Nelson, both Charlie and Carrie had to be treated at the

University of Virginia for exposure and malnutrition before they could be placed in Waynesboro's District Home. The District Home is now closed, but the old site is not far from where I live in Staunton. Carrie and Charlie seemed to find some contentment there. Staff remembered them as a devoted couple, although Carrie was the more active of the pair, and her social worker sometimes worried that she doted on Charlie at the expense of her own health. Caregiving came naturally to her, despite everything she had experienced.

The District Home is now just an empty, derelict building, but its rural setting is one I hope might have pleased her. When she wrote letters to the Colony with messages for Emma, Carrie conveyed that she was well by discussing her garden and animals. "We have a pig and a nice garden and are putting up a lot of things this summer. We have a nice garden spot and tell my mother whenever I can do it I will send her some things. We are pretty hard up now for a good many things but still we are thankful for what we have got in this world."

I drove out to the old District Home in Waynesboro not long ago to remember in place. The day was sunny and warm. The neighboring farms were still putting up their own things for summer. But I was thinking about Christmas.

In 1982, during what was to be her last Christmas, Carrie indulged the staff at the District Home and took on a special role in their holiday program. She embodied a young woman who also rarely speaks in the record that was allowed to her. That woman's words are preserved in the parts of scripture that men like Joseph DeJarnette, during Carrie's trial, probably didn't linger on or produce for biblical flourishes. *He has cast down the mighty from their thrones*, she sings, *and has lifted up the humble.*

Carrie Buck played Mary, a woman held in suspicion and exiled because of the child she was carrying, a child that she eventually lost.

CHAPTER TWO:

MONGREL VIRGINIANS

O n a sunny May day in 1924, white Virginia gathered in Charlottesville to celebrate a momentous occasion for the new South. This South was no longer a fragile thing hiding in the shame of the past, but a living, breathing, modern enterprise that had been secured through an alliance of law, science, education, and above all, power.

After the Civil War, white Southern leaders had suffered the indignity of an arranged marriage. In their eyes, they had swallowed their traditions to be hesitant brides wedded to a disapproving nation. In the intervening decades since the war's end, however, new economies, industries, and institutions helped these visionaries win back the right to claim their own heritage. They were careful to wrap this past in the veneer of future progress in order to achieve what many, even in the North, agreed was a pleasing balance.

On that day in May, 25,000 people pushed out from the campus of the University of Virginia and set a raucous, cheerful course toward downtown. The city's *Daily Progress* called it the "greatest procession which ever threaded the streets of Charlottesville." Military bands, cadets, and soldiers from all corners of the state lent a ceremonial atmosphere to the festivities. Many local businesses had closed for the day.

The most honored guest of all was there only in spirit, hiding in bronze under the shroud of a Confederate flag. But his youngest descendent, a three-year-old named Mary, took over the day's important duties to the best of her ability:

holding a rope, standing tall, receiving cheers. It was the new South distilled in a single moment; delicate life blushing in respectful awe of a rich legacy, an embodied promise built from a bloodline.

A more terrifying, but no less grotesque, kind of pageantry had built to this day of celebration. Just three days prior, the Ku Klux Klan had made their own parade down Main Street, claiming, testing, and expanding the boundaries of this carefully selected gathering place, doing the work that money alone—the very buying of a city— could not achieve. The paper reported, "Thousands lined the sidewalks of Main Street from the C&O Station to the foot of Vinegar Hill." *Vinegar Hill*—the place where Black Charlottesville thrived. Soon, this part of the city would no longer be a threshold, a portal between the worlds of Black and white citizens. It would be a space reserved for white Charlottesville alone.

Edwin Alderman, the president of the University of Virginia, delivered the occasion's most moving remarks, pleasantly blurring the division between town and gown. On this day, all of Charlottesville would receive instruction, in that spot, and so it would be ever after.

"Can you wonder at the measure of the love a people bear for such an embodiment of their best?" Alderman said of their absent honoree. "Surely God was good and full of thought for any people to set at the forefront of their lives so ample a figure, and surely the people of this community may count themselves fortunate in having here before them for all time so glorious a presentment of this serene figure of virtue and greatness." Alderman's words of praise coupled a nostalgia for bygone times with a modern longing, an almost eugenic desire, for the perfect man.

The formal speeches concluded. All eyes returned to Mary, her most important duty yet to come. If stronger hands helped lighten her work, it was not recorded. We only know about the resulting, electrifying connection between old and new, between what had been and what the crowd hoped would forever be.

Mary pulled a rope. The layers of the Confederate flag hiding the ample figure unfolded, revealing the statue of her great-grandfather: Robert E. Lee.

Two months before the unveiling of Charlottesville's Lee statue, Virginia's General Assembly had passed the Racial Integrity Act. The state's Sterilization Act, adopted at the same time, was designed as a culling law. The Racial Integrity Act was a buttressing one. Together, the two laws were designed to protect white racial purity from contamination, both from the outside and from within.

As a buttressing act, Virginia's new law had three specific provisions designed to prevent interracial marriage and reproduction: it required citizens to register their race with the state, it made willful misrepresentation of race a felony, and it newly defined a "white person" as "the person who has no trace whatsoever of any blood other than Caucasian," though there was an exception for people "who have one-sixteenth or less the blood of the American Indian and no other non-Caucasic blood." Native peoples with a blood quantum of more than one-sixteenth became "colored." Thus established, the act resolved that it was "unlawful for any white person in this State to marry save a white person." The final say regarding an individual's racial composition would be determined by Virginia's Bureau of Vital Statistics.

Walter Plecker, the Bureau's head registrar, explained the law's significance to his staff:

> This bill aims at correcting a condition which only the more thoughtful people of Virginia know the existence of . . . It is estimated that there are in the State from 10,000 to 20,000, possibly more, near white people, who are known to possess an intermixture of colored blood, in some cases to a slight extent it is true, but still enough to prevent them from being white.

When Plecker cited those "thoughtful people of Virginia," he was referring to himself. He had been an instrumental figure in the movement to secure the law, which his friend and fellow crusader Earnest Cox praised as "the most perfect expression of the white ideal, and the most important eugenical effort that has been made during the past 4,000 years."

For Plecker and similarly minded zealots, one of the greatest threats to Virginia's social order was lurking in a class of people they often called "mongrels." A eugenic boogeyman like the feebleminded, mongrels were, according to Plecker, "a population combining the worst traits of both conquerors and the conquered." The threat they posed was specific but familiar: each time they reproduced, they not only transmitted defective genes, but also reduced society's ability to see race. And for a society that used racial hierarchy to establish order, that was a problem.

The invention of mongrels took white Virginia's older fears about "white passing" and injected them with eugenic horror. What would happen to society when people who weren't white but looked it could enroll their children in white schools, attend white churches, or move into white neighborhoods? Eugenics helped white Virginians answer that question by moving their doomsday clocks closer to midnight. These mongrels wouldn't just take resources or power, they reasoned, but they would also pollute white bloodlines in irreversible ways.

A mongrel could be anyone eugenicists thought of as the product of interbreeding between races, but for Walter Plecker and his circle of influence, they were always and specifically Native peoples, too. White Virginians had long been hysterical about real and hypothetical breeding between Black and white people. But in Native peoples, eugenicists like Plecker found what they hoped to show was an even deeper abyss: people who were not only biracial, but triracial. Eugenicists reinvented Native peoples as mongrels with an admixture of white, Black, and Native blood. The eugenic logic of the threat they posed worked like this: when interbreeding between two races occurred, the worst traits always became the dominant traits, thus it stood to reason that interbreeding between three races produced an even more pronounced degeneracy.

Policing "amalgamation," the combining of races through reproduction, also made white Virginians more confident in controlling their physical world as well. One outcome implied and desired by the architects of the Racial Integrity Act was a depopulation of "undesirables": both those who had yet to be produced, and those who would assuredly leave the state, or even the country, because they found it so inhospitable. White Virginians also mirrored this intent in the way they ordered their cities, pressing for residential segregation and marking their territory through pageants of violence and the placement of statues.

In the wave of coverage produced after the August 2017 Unite the Right rally, Vann Newkirk's *Atlantic* dispatch from Charlottesville one week after the attacks stands out. Newkirk tried to understand how Black people in Charlottesville were processing the attacks. He found answers in convenience stores, churches, barber shops, and at the University of Virginia. He asked about the city today, and what it was like in the past. No matter where he went, he found the same answer. "What I encountered in Charlottesville wasn't fear," he writes, "but familiarity."

If you want to understand the creation of Virginia's Racial Integrity Act, one of your first ports of call will be the Albert and Shirley Small Special Collections at the University of Virginia. Once there, you should ask for the papers of John Powell, a once celebrated UVA alumnus who, along with fellow travelers Walter Plecker and Earnest Cox, formed Virginia's premier society for the defense of racial integrity in 1922.

The guide to this archival collection will explain that Powell was "a world-renowned pianist and composer who was born in Richmond, Virginia, on September 6, 1882." Powell's brief biography is longest where it details his musical achievements. But what else did he do? In the biography's last paragraph, there it is: "He was considered by many to be the 'founding father of racial integrity legislation in Virginia.'"

As his biography indicates, Powell was not a politician. He was more of a desperately racist influencer, a figure whose celebrity became a kind of propaganda in its own right. Born into an elite Virginia family, he, like many of his peers, came to nurture a toxic obsession with the past. But where leaders like Alderman restored themselves in the shadows of Lee and Stonewall Jackson, Powell's obsession reflected a more complicated outlook.

He believed, like any spoiled child might, that he was the best boy of all. His talents? Unmatched. His sophistication? Unparalleled. His wealth? Elite. His pedigree? Superb. But in Powell's mind, his background was also indicative of an increasingly unhinged proposition that the world's best genetic specimens were revenants of an ancient race—the purest of the pure who were worthy of additional exaltation.

Powell's position as a member of Virginia's elite whites

wasn't enough to satisfy him, so he fashioned himself Anglo-Saxon as well, an heir to the genius of ancient conquerors and civilization builders. The thesis of his genetic origins applied mythical understandings of the past to underscore the Anglo-Saxons' role as the custodian of all virtues. In Powell's formulation, they were the creators of laws and the preservers of liberty. But they were also a brawny and virile subgroup that wasn't afraid to get their hands dirty through violence and conquest when it was required.

Did it dilute Powell's genetic potency to be on American soil? Not at all. If anything, his ancestors' migration had been a saving grace by protecting strains of Anglo-Saxon stock from being contaminated by lesser Europeans. To Powell's dismay, these lesser folks, like eastern European Jews, now happened to be immigrating to America in record numbers. While everyone Powell respected wouldn't have necessarily shared his unique genetic claim, he was sure they could collectively agree to, or otherwise fall in line with, a set of common values he would determine based upon his own superior pedigree. Powell, in other words, believed in a master race.

And he was not alone. He was an acolyte of naturalist Madison Grant, the author of 1916's *The Passing of the Great Race*. Perhaps more than anyone else of his time, it was Grant who set the tone for scientific racism's great cultural rise, not just because of what he believed, but how he was able to articulate it.

Grant was a viper's viper, a man with a sharp and poisonous center who possessed great wealth and the credentials of a well-established family. His center of power was New York City, where he watched the metropolis grow with new immigrants while he also indulged his scientific passions at the New York Zoological Park (now the Bronx Zoo). Grant was admired by many early conservationists for his theories of wildlife management, by which I mean he believed, in a nod to the eugenicist he would become, that the best animals should be preserved so that the best men could enjoy hunting them. He also sometimes advocated that African men be put in cages, on display among the animals.

Ian Frazier, writing in 2019 for the *New Yorker*, points out that this portrait of Grant was the "better" version of him; the human-zoo-having, save-the-animals-just-to-shoot-them naturalist of the Teddy Roosevelt variety. "But," Frazier warns, "like a character in a comic book who harbors an inner arch-villain with a plan to destroy the universe, Grant had another side."

This other side of Grant often argued, as it did in *The Passing of the Great Race*, that "the Laws of Nature require the obliteration of the unfit." But who were the unfit? Grant suggested that any answers to this question must follow a single path that sprang from answering another: who are the fittest? He believed the most superior race to be the Nordic people, of whom Anglo-Saxons were a subtype. If there are "badly beaten races" as any eugenicist might suggest, there had to be a race that beat them. In this formulation, other people who might look white but who were of non-Nordic origins (like Italians) became the carriers of "peasant character," still surviving as a race "but greatly impaired." By contrast, Nordics were "a race of soldiers, sailors, adventurers, and explorers, but above all, of rulers, organizers, and aristocrats." Adam Serwer, in the *Atlantic*, writes, "Grant blended Nordic boosterism with fearmongering, and supplied a scholarly veneer for notions that many white citizens already wanted to believe." His ideas fit seamlessly into a society that felt it was under attack from immigrants, Black people, and low-life whites.

Calling Grant a scientific racist—as the description of beliefs that use pseudoscience to prove white racial superiority—is accurate based on our contemporary use of the term, but it is also very generous. Like his fan John

Powell, the underpinnings of Grant's ideas were an incoherent mess, cobbled together from plagiarized ideas. It would be a good insult, using a language Powell and Grant would have understood, to call their theories mongrelized, the worst parts of already bad ideas. But those same ideas were also extremely popular. By World War II, *The Passing of the Great Race* had gone through thirteen printings over four editions, including one special copy that Adolf Hitler called his Bible.

Jonathan Spiro, Grant's biographer, writes, "like a spider perched in the middle of its increasingly intricate web . . . Grant lay in his bed in Manhattan and used the telephone, telegraph, and the U.S. mail to masterfully coordinate the activities of the interlocking directorate of scientific racism." By 1924, Grant and his acolytes were taking credit for the country's new restrictive immigration policies.

Ivey Forman Lewis, a biologist who became the dean of the University of Virginia's College of Arts and Sciences in 1946, wrote about Grant's enduring legacy. In letters later found by Gregory Dorr, Lewis wrote to a colleague, "There is no biological principle better established than that of inequality of races, and yet sociologists, especially the Jewish ones, are loud and effective in their denial of any racial differences, even saying there is no such thing as race. They deride and laugh to scorn such books as Madison Grant's 'Passing of the Great Race.'"

John Powell's own esteem of Grant's master race propaganda went through several phases, including a musical one. His most famous composition, *Rhapsodie Negre*, which premiered in 1922, explores the subordination of Africa's "genuine primitives" to "Caucasian civilization." He dedicated its debut to Joseph Conrad, a contemporary writer who drew deeply from myths of Africa as the "Dark Continent," most famously in 1899's *Heart of Darkness*. In the biographical note Powell included in the program, he credentialed himself as the founder of the University of Virginia's Society for the Preservation of Racial Integrity.

In 1922, at the peak of his musical celebrity, Powell founded the Anglo-Saxon Clubs of America in Richmond, Virginia. The plural "Clubs" and the "America" part were a bit aspirational, but that was very on-brand for him. It was to be an organization for the thinking man's racist, people too wealthy or intellectual to play well with the Ku Klux Klan. The Anglo-Saxon Clubs would also not be a secret fraternity. Instead, it would be filled with men who put their credentials, and their stock, front and center for admiration. Learning from Grant, but also from his own fame, Powell appreciated the power of propaganda and the benefits of an organization with a strong inner circle.

His earliest allies included Walter Plecker of the Bureau of Vital Statistics and Earnest Sevier Cox, a Richmond transplant who had recently authored a piece of Madison Grant fan fiction entitled *White America*. Plecker, a physician by training, became Virginia's first registrar of vital statistics in 1912. From Augusta County, Virginia, he was the son of a Confederate veteran and had established his worldview from the arrangement of life and labor in his slave-owning family. He often claimed, using that peculiar logic of the Old South, that his racist schemes were intended to benefit Black people as well as white. Black people would always be inferior to white people, his reasoning went, but by submitting to the corrective influence of their betters, they might be taught to make improvements within their own race.

Earnest Cox was a racial separatist and a cruder version of Grant. Outside Richmond, he acted as a white ambassador for Marcus Garvey's United Negro Improvement Association, a pan-African organization that was, in this era, soliciting financial support to send Black people in the United States to Africa as a form of repatriation. Cox was also a real estate agent, a Methodist preacher, and a world traveler. His passion for solving racial problems had been inspired by his years living in South Africa and observing what he felt was a beneficial relationship between the colonized and their colonizers.

The trio made quite an alliance. Powell, of course, was the charismatic celebrity whose convictions and charms worked magic for the cause. Bookish Plecker worked diligently behind the scenes, constructing worlds of statistical nightmares and deploying a eugenicist's hysterical math to accentuate the organization's claims of race suicide. Cox flavored his duties with fire and brimstone—apparently he was a better speaker than a writer—and his opportunistic friendships with Black separatists lent a false nobility to Powell's circle. *Here are fine, solution-focused men*, the world could think, *and not one of them too proud to reach across the color line when needs must*.

As one of Richmond's most famous citizens, Powell had a friendly relationship with the city's white press. In 1923, the *Richmond Times-Dispatch* allowed the Anglo-Saxon Clubs prime space in its Sunday magazine to ask, "Is White America to Become a Negroid Nation?" This roller coaster of a question lifted white Virginians to terrifying heights before dropping them back down on the solid earth of a fine solution. Virginia needed the strongest anti-race mixing and racial purity laws it could possibly pass, Powell argued. He later justified the proposition in terms that would have been familiar to Virginia's white vanguard but was carried further with eugenic thought: "one drop of negro blood makes the negro is no longer a theory based on race pride or color prejudice, but a logically induced scientific fact." Powell, Plecker, and Cox tag-teamed Richmond's press throughout the summer of 1923; Powell and Cox wrote fearmongering editorials, and Plecker sometimes shared his similar views in a follow-up that explained how the Bureau could be of use to the project.

As Virginia's 1924 legislative session drew near, endorsements for the type of law proposed by the Anglo-Saxon Clubs increased. The *Times-Dispatch* and the *Richmond News Leader* both endorsed the club's objectives, as did the reliable cadre of famous white nationalists, including Madison Grant. "It would, of course, be a frightful calamity not only to the South but the whole nation—in fact to civilization, itself—if the struggle for the supremacy of the white race were in any degree diminished," Grant wrote in support. "It is the insidious increase of mixed breeds in the lower strata of society which has heretofore undermined and ruined many white civilizations."

A version of the bill passed into law in March 1924. The spirit of the law reflected the provisions demanded by the Anglo-Saxon Clubs with one important difference. The law that was initially proposed had deeply offended members of Virginia's powerful and aristocratic class by inadvertently questioning their genetic credentials; a number of Virginia's most elite white families claimed to be descendants of a woman named Matoaka, but who they called Pocahontas. Under the hard-line, "one-drop" rule first proposed, her descendants would become "colored"—a frightful calamity, as Madison Grant might say. The law was ultimately amended to allow a so-called "Pocahontas Exception." White persons with a quantum of one-sixteenth or less "Indian blood" would remain white in the eyes of the state.

For Walter Plecker, the Racial Integrity Act was the high point of his career. It was perhaps his lowest, too. The Pocahontas Exception created what he felt was a dangerous loophole. It was all but assured, he imagined, that mongrels would attempt to exploit it in order to become white in the official eyes of Virginia. In pursuit of its closure, he waged a campaign that Chief William Miles of the Pamunkey Tribe would later describe as "statistical genocide." Using the power of an office that touched every life in the state, Plecker created a false genealogical record of Virginia's Native peoples that would eventually allow him to boast, "Hitler's genealogical study of the Jews is not more complete."

After 1924, in the world that all Virginians passed through as they were born, married, and died, Native peoples did not exist. What existed instead were "colored" people who claimed to be Indian. It's not that Plecker, the architect of this world, denied the fact that the United States was populated by Native peoples before white settlers arrived. But his argument was that, over time, those groups had descended into mongrelization, interbreeding with white, but more often with Black, people.

How people self-identified was no concern to Plecker. To him, that was an annoying habit that people of lesser genetic stock employed to sneak privileges that should be set aside for white people. The federal government, for example, allowed Native peoples to list their race as "Indian" when registering for military service. This exempted them from serving in a segregated unit and allowed them to fight alongside white soldiers. Loopholes like this, along with Virginia's Pocahontas Exception, set Plecker's teeth on edge.

His irritations and fears often focused on two mountainous, neighboring counties, Amherst and Rockbridge, located at the southern end of the Shenandoah Valley near Lexington. Much of this area today is made up of the occupied lands of the Monacan Indian Nation. This includes Bear Mountain, where the Monacan tribal museum now sits on a former mission site. In 1925, Plecker wrote, "The Amherst-Rockbridge group of about 800 similar people are giving us the most trouble, through actual numbers and persistent claims of being Indians. Some well-meaning church workers have established an 'Indian Mission' around which they rally." By that point, he was well on his way to compiling what Virginia's Native peoples have called his "hit list," a compilation of surnames Plecker believed were common among troublesome, "colored" Virginians, particularly those, like the "Amherst-Rockbridge group," that he felt would attempt to pass as white.

Plecker's New Year's message in 1943, for example, warned local registrars to expect a "rush to register as white" among Native peoples. Admittedly, he was always warning about this, but he was particularly concerned in this moment because Native peoples were trying to refuse registering for the draft as "Negro." To help his local departments spot these "mongrels," as he called them, he provided a list of surnames "of mixed negroid Virginia families striving to pass as 'Indian' or white." In Amherst County, for example, he warned of families with these names:

> Adcock (Adcox), Beverly (this family is now trying to evade the situation by adopting the name Burch or Birch, which was the name of the white mother of the present generation), Branham, Duff, Floyd, Hamilton, Hartless, Hicks, Johns, Lawless, Nickles (Knuckles), Painter, Ramsey, Redcross, Roberts, Southards (Suthards, Southerds, Southers), Sorrells, Terry, Tyree, Willis, Clark, Cash, Wood.

He later added, "One hundred and fifty thousand other mulattoes in Virginia are watching eagerly the attempt of their pseudo-Indian brethren, ready to follow in a rush when the first have made a break in the dike."

In *Segregation's Science*, Gregory Dorr describes how Plecker's "devotion to racial integrity approached the monomaniacal. He threatened midwives and mothers. He patrolled cemeteries, segregating graves and defending the racial integrity of the Old Dominion's corpses." Plecker's methods were brutal and effective. The world was as he said it was, even if that meant changing the vital records of people born contemporaneously in Virginia and altering the records of those long dead.

Plecker's specific fixation on Rockbridge and Amherst Counties was connected to a number of ideas and grievances. That the mountains were filled with defective people, due to isolation and inbreeding, was already a well-established eugenic talking point. Plecker, as he explains in his letters, also found the "persistent claims of being Indians" there distressing. He had also grown up just over the mountain in Augusta County, about thirty miles away. Perhaps because his worldview first formed in that part of the state, he always wanted to remake it in his image.

Rockbridge County had also been the site of an early and humiliating defeat for him. In 1924, a Virginia judge overturned his decision to deny a marriage license to a young woman, Atha Sorrells, and her fiancé; Plecker and his local registrar had argued that, under the new Racial Integrity Act, Sorrells was colored and her fiancé was white. This was news to the Sorrells family, and the dispute ended up in the Rockbridge County Court.

According to the Sorrells family, every Sorrells in living memory was white, had been accepted as white, and imagined that they looked white. They had attended white schools and white churches. The new law, however, gave Plecker room to create policy around his pet theories, and he believed that miscegenation was common among families who were settled in the South River community, where the Sorrells lived. He claimed to have documents that proved Atha Sorrells had "negro blood." The Sorrells, however, claimed they had a

Native ancestor who likely had been misclassified as Virginia moved away from defining people only as white, free (Black), or slave. In other words, the Sorrells claimed the Pocahontas Exception that roiled Plecker.

The Sorrells won their case, largely because the judge, Henry W. Holt, lost the plot. Plecker overcomplicated the matter with elaborate family trees, antiquarian bullshit, and a personality that favored preaching about the dangers of race-mixing over clarifying the facts at hand. While Plecker was on the stand, Holt calculated how many ancestors he might have himself. "In twenty-five generations," he later explained in his verdict, "one has thirty-two millions of grandfathers not to speak of grandmothers, assuming there is no intermarriage." He wondered if it was necessary, past a certain point, to know them all intimately.

Judge Holt is not a hero in this story, however. He is simply a white Southerner of a more realistic outlook. Although he expressed his "cordial sympathy" with Plecker's goal, it was not worth investing resources and invoking the power of the state to pick apart the bloodlines of harmless people who had long been accepted as white. If anything, such aggression might harm the overall cause. Malicious enforcement might result in the overturning of a law that was otherwise useful.

Plecker was outraged at the verdict. He enlisted Powell to fire off a warning shot in the form of a pamphlet titled *The Breach in the Dike: An Analysis of the Sorrels* [sic] *Case, Showing the Danger to Racial Integrity from Intermarriage of Whites with So-called Indians.* Producing their favorite blunt object, the dike metaphor, Powell and company warned, "If we are to preserve our civilization, our ideals, the soul of our race, we must call a halt" to white-passing in all its forms. In private, however, Plecker accepted Holt's decision. He might have appealed the ruling to a higher court, but decided it was not worth the risk of potentially weakening the law further if he lost again. "Our hope is to drift along until the next legislature, and have them pass a bill preventing the marriage of the Indians with the whites," he wrote to one of his registrars.

In this hope, Plecker had what he thought of as an ace up his sleeve. He was aware that one of the Eugenic Record Office's best fieldworkers was writing a new book about this part of Virginia. Its release, Plecker reasoned, would not only yield additional ammunition for his crusade, but also lift his cause using the reputations of leaders in the national movement.

Mountain or rural primitivism has always offered endless inspiration for shitty writers. This fact is as true today as it was in the era of eugenics. But back then, colorful stories about mountaineers or rural folk frozen in time back in the hills transformed, without much remodeling, into rumors about defective people. Eugenicists considered these people to be cacogenic, from the Greek *kakos*, meaning "bad." And cacogenic families, eugenicists believed, were living evidence of a broader genetic deterioration taking place over time.

After the 1877 publication of Richard Dugdale's *The Jukes: A Study of Crime, Pauperism, Disease and Heredity*, family studies became something of a bread and butter trade for eugenic fieldworkers. Dugdale's examination of a "hill family" from upstate New York contained estimates that a single family had produced, since their patriarch's arrival to America in the early eighteenth century, several hundred welfare recipients and dozens of convicted criminals, prostitutes, and brothel-keepers. He claimed they had collectively cost the state of New York well over a million dollars.

Dugdale's work provided a powerful model of the kind of research that both public and private entities, from prison associations to the Rockefeller family, were willing to fund. By 1916, Arthur Estabrook, a fieldworker for the Eugenics Record Office, had rewritten Dugdale's study to emphasize the role of defective genes. He also updated the costs associated with the Juke family's dependency to over two million dollars.

In 1923, the Eugenics Record Office sent Estabrook to Amherst County, Virginia, to conduct research into a rumored "lost tribe" living in the Blue Ridge Mountains. His initial tip came from Harvey Jordan, a eugenicist at the University of Virginia who in 1939 became dean of its College of Medicine. The University of Virginia, however, was not involved in Estabrook's research on this particular subject when the project began to materialize a decade later. Instead, Estabrook partnered with Sweet Briar College, a rural women's institution in Amherst County located right in the backyard of the research study's target area.

Estabrook partnered with Sweet Briar professor Ivan McDougle to conduct the study and serve as a local guide. McDougle was someone the Eugenics Record Office considered an ally in the academy. He brought eugenics into Sweet Briar's curriculum just after his arrival in 1918 and set a course to have it incorporated through the college's sociology offerings. This made him an attractive collaborator to the Eugenics Record Office. But he also had something more important to offer—access to dozens and dozens of young white women who were eager to do student training in eugenic fieldwork.

Young white women, like the kind McDougle was able to recruit, were a special asset to eugenic fieldwork. Field research required tedious errands—poring over birth certificates and marriage records, constructing elaborate genetic maps— but it also involved home visits and face-to-face interviews with population groups that had been predetermined to be cacogenic. Young and keen white women were often more successful at persuading individuals to volunteer information about their health and family histories, to allow fieldworkers to see their babies, and to offer clues about more intimate subjects like marriage and sex. Leaders at the Eugenic Record Office talked up their women researchers, telling them that their female sensitivity made them better detectors of bad genes. Once successfully trained, these young women would become welfare officers, social workers, and even teachers. Although far from the nerve center of the national movement in New York, the women of Sweet Briar College also had the Lynchburg Colony in their backyard as the perfect site for practicing fieldwork.

A photograph taken of McDougle's four-person team offers another hint that yielding the more intimate interviews to women workers was a smart move by eugenicists. In it, three young women recline in a grassy spot, beaming. It's almost like a yearbook photo, a moment intended to convey youth and potential, the anticipation of many more sunny days. But that illusion is shattered by the awkward and hulking figure of a bow-tied McDougle in the background, the very image of an aloof professor. Puffed out and wide-armed, he has decided to pose on his knees to achieve some height over the women instead of sitting with them in the grass. It's not hard to imagine how many rural Virginia families would prefer to confide personal information with the young women.

According to rumor and local lore, the "lost tribe" at the center of the study had become lost through intermarriage between both Black and white outsiders. The fieldworkers' task was to determine this tribe's precise origins and quantify its genetic reach. From these facts, a trail of invisible contamination could be produced. Despite couching their research as the discovery of a lost tribe, the researchers were simply targeting Monacan Indians, along with some of their eugenically questionable white and Black neighbors. They knew this. The community knew this too; Sweet Briar students had even occasionally worked at the Monacan mission.

Their study eventually became *Mongrel Virginians: The Win Tribe*, which was published in 1926. "Win" was an acronym that stood for "white-Indian-negro." The name was useful to researchers because it described a population group they believed to be triracial. Making the tribe anonymous also helped enhance the researchers' sense of ownership over the study. As a happy bonus, it would also make their findings more difficult to challenge.

Estabrook and McDougle positioned the Wins as a group of "mixed bloods" who were considered by the local population to be "neither white nor negro." "The Wins themselves," the researchers sigh at one point, "claim to be of Indian descent."

Mongrel Virginians is required reading for anyone who assumes that eugenicists, ever preoccupied with intelligence, operated under sharp intellectual standards for their own work. The study contains over two dozen genealogical case studies filled with repetitive, vicious descriptions. The Wins are uneducated. The Wins are promiscuous. The Wins are universally lazy, ill-tempered, and unattractive. The Wins come in every hue, from pale to copper to dark-skinned.

Estabrook and McDougle appear to have exhausted themselves by creating hundreds of pseudonyms, and, perhaps washed out, they relied on a very short list of adjectives in their descriptions, their favorite of which is "typical": "He was a typical Indian, a renter, and amounted to nothing;" "He is a typical mixture, short, kinky hair now becoming grey, medium dark complexion, flat nose, a typical mulatto type;" "He is a typical Win, unintelligent and very stubborn in make-up;" "She is a typical Indian type with dark complexion and dark hair, very defective mentally." Given their enthusiasm for this descriptor, it is fair to note that their typical way of signaling an important fact is by prefacing it with the phrase, "legend has it."

The book received an uneven reception from the broader scientific community. The *Journal of Applied Psychology*, for example, complimented the researchers for "yielding valuable data" and "calling attention to a problem of serious social inadequacy." Eugenicists were confident that their prolific fieldwork, which could demonstrably shape law and policy, had definitively resolved the nature/nurture debate in their favor.

But some experts were alarmed at the eugenicists' overblown conclusions and the way they'd let power go to their heads. In the *Annals of the American Academy*, Abraham Myerson, a neurologist with a long career working in senior positions in psychiatric hospitals and who later became Massachusetts state forensic examiner, called *Mongrel Virginians* "a really absurd and useless book!" Let me type that out again: "a really absurd and useless book!" Exclamation. He reviewed the text as nothing more than "the most trifling morsels of gossip, with arbitrary interpretations, with no possibility of verification since many of the characters are dead." Were Estabrook and McDougle never boy scouts, Myerson wondered? Surely not if they got this twisted up at the very idea of Indians.

But wait, you might be thinking, *Native peoples no longer existed on paper in Virginia.* Wouldn't the researchers' findings, and all this talk about "typical Indians," complicate things for Virginia in the age of its Racial Integrity Law? In some ways, yes. Here is the difference between a eugenicist like Walter Plecker and one like Arthur Estabrook, though. For someone like Plecker, the world was literally black and white. No other categories were needed. The Eugenics Record Office, however, saw beyond those distinctions. Put bluntly, one-drop rules produced a kind of social order that eugenicists, who were often white supremacists, supported. But those rules also took the fun out of eugenic science, flattening some of the pleasure that came with being smart about these things. Thinking of racial variation as a math problem, a eugenicist like Plecker would quickly and arrogantly jot down the answer, knowing it well in advance. Estabrook and McDougle, on the other hand, took pleasure in showing their work.

Mongrel Virginians tried to split the difference in some ways. The authors published the full text of the Racial Integrity Act as an appendix while also concluding with a disclaimer stating, "Amidst the furor of newspaper and pamphlet publicity on miscegenation which has appeared since the passage of the Racial Integrity Law of 1924 this study is presented not as theory or as representing a prejudiced point of view but as a careful summary of the facts of history." At the end of the day, researchers suggested, there was something worse than being colored, and that was being a mongrel. A mongrel keeps no company but his own kind. And his own kind are a composite of genetic and moral failures, a "badly put together people" as Charles Davenport, the director of the Eugenics Record Office, might call them. This conclusion happily fed the egos of both science-minded eugenicists and race-baiters alike.

If that line at the conclusion of *Mongrel Virginians* about the furor of pamphlets was a dig at Plecker, who got in trouble for sending over sixty thousand pamphlets of his personal writing out in the world using taxpayer money, he didn't seem to care. Besides, he wanted Estabrook's raw data to beef up his hit list. Estabrook collegially refused the request. Eugenicists were usually a fairly content stepfamily, so the researchers' dislike of Plecker is notable. In "Disability, Eugenics, and the Culture Wars," Paul Lombardo explains: "in the ocean of ideas, eugenics was a bottom feeder, taking whatever it needed to make the case against social welfare programs, expensive institutions, and the people who lived in them." But Plecker's circle was so outspoken in their white nationalism, so uncaring about how their more scientific brethren needed the world to work, that it started to kill the mood. Some grumbled about

Plecker privately. The eugenics movement had its dispassionate, scientific veneer, and then it had Plecker, who was trying to get the bodies of people who were now "colored" exhumed from white cemeteries.

Plecker died in 1947 when he was hit by a car as he was crossing the road in Richmond. His plans to use his retirement to write books in the style of Madison Grant happily died with him. At first, it was slightly difficult for me to learn the truth about Plecker's death. It had become a mythologized event, and understandably so, among his victims. In some tellings, Plecker had developed such an inflated sense of arrogance that he believed even traffic would instantly stop for him. Some versions start with a prequel—an anecdote about a woman who Plecker had assaulted years previously after she saved him from being run over by a car. "He laid her out like she'd touched God," someone who lived in his neighborhood remembered. Sometimes the car in the story isn't a car, but a bus, and the driver is Native. The headline to his death announcement in the *Richmond Afro-American* read, "Dr. Plecker, 86, Rabid Racist, Killed by Auto." "We mention his passing here," the paper explained, "not to mourn him but to applaud the fact that race haters of his type are leaving the scene."

One of the most immediate consequences of Plecker's actions, and work like *Mongrel Virginians*, was a decrease in the Native population across Virginia. We know this because the federal government still used "Indian" as a census category at this time, and also because this migration from Virginia is a story told in many Native families today. Historian Melanie Haimes-Bartloff finds that "in 1948, only 326 individuals remained at the Bear Mountain Mission community after intense racism motivated more than two hundred Bear Mountain Monacans with resources to leave for Maryland, New Jersey, and Tennessee."

Part of Plecker's work was undone by *Loving v. Virginia*, the

1967 Supreme Court case that struck down laws nationwide that banned interracial marriage. But in September 2019, six plaintiffs filed suit against the state in order to challenge a law still on the books in Virginia stating that couples seeking a marriage license must report their race. The set of plaintiffs, who reside in Rockbridge County, claimed the clerk provided them with a list of choices that included "octaroon" and "teutonic." In response to the lawsuit, the state's attorney general, Mark Herring, quickly issued new marriage certificate forms that indicated reporting race is voluntary. Herring's new instructions, however, did not change the underlying law and in fact contradicted it, meaning that a future attorney general could simply reverse the practice and make reporting race mandatory again. In October 2019, ninety-five years after Virginia passed its Racial Integrity Act, the United States District Court for the Eastern District of Virginia ruled that the law violated the Fourteenth Amendment and was a "vestige of the nation's and Virginia's history of codified racialization."

Karenne Wood, a member of the Monacan Indian Nation and the former long-serving director of the Virginia Indian Programs at Virginia Humanities, once called Walter Plecker "the villain in our sacred story." The Monacan Indian Nation, along with the Chickahominy Indian Tribe, the Chickahominy Indian Tribe-Eastern Division, the Upper Mattaponi Tribe, the Rappahannock Tribe, and the Nansemond Indian Tribe, struggled for decades to achieve federal recognition due to Virginia's past erasures. Some members have spoken of individual ways they were able to subvert Plecker's ultimate goal, by preserving or finding their kin or rejoining communities later in life. In Amherst County, for example, the Bear Mountain Mission School continued to serve Monacan children and support their Native identities. But their bureaucratic invisibility hampered their collective ability to produce the type of documentation that was necessary to follow the federal process set by the Department of the Interior's Bureau of Indian Affairs.

As Stephen Adkins, Chief of the Chickahominy Tribe, explained to Congress in 2005, Virginia's laws and Plecker's actions were tantamount to cultural genocide for Virginia's Native peoples. "I have persevered in this process for one reason," Adkins said of the path to federal recognition, "I do not want my family or my tribe to let the legacy of Walter Plecker stand." In 2007, the same year that Virginia celebrated the four-hundred-year anniversary of the arrival of European settlers, this attempt to bring collective recognition to the six tribes by special legislation failed in the Senate.

But in 2018, Virginia Senators Tim Kaine and Mark Warner were able to bring forward a successful vote. The Thomasina E. Jordan Indian Tribe of Virginia Federal Recognition Act was signed into law in January 2018. Had I written this book slightly earlier, I would not be able to supply this update. That is how unsettled the history of eugenics remains, how firmly it sits atop the lives of people here and now.

———————

Today, I can do something that Walter Plecker probably never imagined in his wildest dreams—leave my house and purchase a commercial test at most pharmacies that purports the ability to read my DNA. I have never done this, but I know that, as a white person, I have nothing to fear if my genetic profile suggests that I share ancestries with nonwhite people. On the contrary, for some white people, the potential for those results is part of the test's allure. In 2018, Massachusetts Senator Elizabeth Warren took heat for using DNA testing to "prove" her Cherokee ancestry, a long-claimed facet of her biography that has frequently been criticized by Native peoples for legitimizing what some call "Cherokee syndrome":

the appropriation of Native identity on the basis of tenuous evidence like family legends without understanding concepts like sovereignty, citizenship, and the right of tribes to determine their own members.

Rebecca Nagle, a Cherokee Nation citizen, explains that claims like Warren's, made on the basis of DNA test results or just family myths, force Native peoples to relive racist stereotypes. Appropriation makes it acceptable to ask Native peoples, for example, "What part Cherokee are you?" The demand for an answer is one part of the insult. But more broadly, those questions and claims run contrary to the way that Native nations define their own sovereignty and instead make identity a question of parts, just as racial composition laws once did. "We are living, real, and whole people; not fractions of Indians who used to be real," Nagle said.

For people who do not face intrusive relationships with others or with state power because of their race, the idea of being fractions can be pleasurable. In cases where white people have used DNA testing to claim their businesses are now minority-owned enterprises, it can even be profitable. Researchers Wendy Roth and Biorn Ivemark found, in a study they released through the *American Journal of Sociology* in 2018, that white people were more likely than nonwhite people to adopt or even cherry-pick new identities from commercial DNA testing results.

Roth suggests a theory called "optimal distinctiveness" might be at work; someone who belongs to a majority might want to try on minority identities to increase their own uniqueness. But if that theory is too abstract, there is always white guilt. In an interview with *MEL Magazine*, Roth also conceded that "some of them," meaning white people in the study's sample, "might have had a bit of guilt—white guilt about being privileged in society. And being able to claim a non-European identity might have helped them deal with some of that guilt. Or at least ignore it."

But in the world of whiteness and DNA testing, there is something more than appropriation happening. Walter Plecker could not have envisioned commercial DNA testing, but he might have appreciated the ways that it has, to some degree, revived the eugenic proposition that who we are is written into our genes. Only now, white supremacists are caught in the crossfire. In July 2019, Joan Donovan and Aaron Panofsky, technology and public policy researchers, released the findings of a study concerning the white supremacist online community Stormfront. Donovan and Panofsky were interested to know if the modern phenomenon of commercial DNA testing and the deeper ancestral understandings it claims to impart were complicating things for the group, which requires members to be "100% white."

The two researchers had noticed a phenomenon in which members enlisted DNA testing to help them prove their genetic credentials. Sometimes this yielded results the members considered disastrous. "I am 58% European, 29% Native American, and 13% Middle Eastern," read one post the researchers provided. "I am pretty sure Middle Eastern is Caucasian too . . . so it means I am 71% Caucasian?" the poster hoped.

Donovan and Panofsky's work builds interesting layers and important details into an unsurprising conclusion: white supremacists are full of shit, and they use whatever understandings and myths that are most convenient to them in the service of their repressive goals. I am not insulting the study at all, or the sophisticated ways the authors found to present this truth. If anything, it is good to hear, as Panofsky warned the *New York Times*, that "science cannot save us." But complicating the ways that white supremacists understand whiteness, even their own whiteness, is a zero-sum game that could just as likely produce a belief that commercial DNA testing is a Jewish plot as it could a moment of profound reflection.

For past eugenicists, the most exciting part of their scientific ambitions was rarely the science itself; it was the subsequent degradation of the legitimacy of others. Eugenicists had all the same weaknesses they condemned in others—disabilities, less-than-pure genetic stock, reputations for promiscuity. Many of them did not have the large, fit families they demanded from other good, white Americans. In one of the most damning but wholly predictable exchanges between Plecker and Powell, Plecker jokes about being warned that he might face continued legal troubles for haphazardly changing people's races: "In reality I have been doing a good deal of bluffing, knowing all the while it could not ever be legally sustained." The punchline, of course, is that Plecker's ideas often were sustained. A minor rebuke here or there wasn't much of a losing proposition, except for those people Plecker was targeting.

In 1916, Charlottesville's *Daily Progress* reported on the city's recent Halloween parade, finding one particular moment most enjoyable: "a gay battalion of Ku Klux Klan came thundering down from the heights of the Midway, recalling other days. Many a dusky denizen of the 'bottom' was seen to shrink instinctively back into the shadows of Preston Avenue." That the *Daily Progress* found this battalion "gay" is likely connected to the fact that these Klan members were not adults, but children in their Halloween costumes. It amused white observers to watch these children get their first taste of making Black citizens shrink back into the shadows in fear.

Today, if you try to follow the route of this parade, you'll wind about a mile through Charlottesville's downtown mall and end up at a Staples store awkwardly plopped just at the fringes of the downtown core. There, just beyond the Staples, the only landmark that conveys something of Charlottesville's past in an easily discernible way is a school that went up in 1926. This is the Jefferson School—now a community center—which was created to be one of only ten Black high schools in Virginia. The little parading Klan members in 1916 wouldn't have caught sight of the Robert E. Lee statue because its placement was still eight years in the future; though perhaps by the time it went up in 1924, some of those children had become the young men who took the same parade route.

In 1916, cities like Charlottesville, which had passed "An Ordinance to Secure for White and Colored People a Separate Location of Residence for Each Race" in 1912, had their futures in the hands of a legal challenge making its way to the Supreme Court. This case, originating from Louisville, Kentucky, would decide if government-instituted racial segregation in residential areas was constitutional. Charlottesville's ordinance had stated that a Black person occupying a home in a predominately white neighborhood (or vice versa) could be punished with a fine or a minimum of thirty days in jail. In 1917, the Supreme Court ruled that those ordinances violated the Fourteenth Amendment because they prevented white people from disposing of their property how they saw fit. If a white person wanted to sell a property to a Black person, the Supreme Court ruled, that was his constitutionally protected right.

The Supreme Court, however, took pains to clarify:

> It is the purpose of such enactments, and, it is frankly avowed, it will be their ultimate effect, to require by law, at least in residential districts, the compulsory separation of the races on account of color. Such action is said to be essential to maintain

> the purity of the races. . . . The case presented does not deal with an attempt to prohibit the amalgamation of the races. The right to which the ordinance annulled was the civil right of a white man to dispose of his property if he saw fit to do so to a person of color.

In other words, the Supreme Court explained that it understood such ordinances had been motivated by a desire to maintain racial purity, and that its ruling should not be seen as obstructive to the broad aim of preventing amalgamation. By amalgamation, it meant, similar to miscegenation, the combining of races through procreation. In 1924, Virginia would create its Racial Integrity Act as its most explicit method of prevention.

The Supreme Court ruling meant that Charlottesville had to devise new ways to contain Black people geographically in order to preserve racial purity. The city leveraged other types of zoning ordinances, encouraged private contracts that produced segregation through deed restriction, manipulated the placement of utilities, and marked territory by Klan parades and, eventually, Confederate statues. But concentrating Black people into one area of the city also risked an outcome that white city leaders did not enjoy thinking about, either: that Black people would invest in their neighborhoods, find ways to grow their communities, and pass some generational wealth to their children. Limiting this potential meant restricting education, healthcare, employment, and income for Black people in Charlottesville as well. A study commissioned by the Charlottesville Low-Income Housing Coalition in 2020 found that after 1948, when the Supreme Court ruled that racial covenants were unconstitutional, the city "increased economically restrictive zoning as a proxy for explicit racial restrictions" to an extent so great that these same zoning practices now impede the city's ability to grow.

In the 1960s, the Preston Avenue area where Klan-robed children had once frightened Black people "back into the shadows" became part of the target area for a city beautification campaign. Just a decade prior, the Supreme Court had affirmed the government's right to utilize eminent domain solely for the purpose of beautification and redevelopment. In 1960, the mayor of Charlottesville, Thomas Mitchie, looked out at Preston Avenue and its larger Vinegar Hill neighborhood and concluded, "we are fortunate that the worst slum area in the city lends itself beautifully to plans for urban renewal." What Mitchie found fortunate about this arrangement was that what he called a slum was located on property that was valuable to the city. The economic and physical growth of the city's downtown was stagnating as suburbanization pushed residents and their business enterprises further out to the fringes of the city.

Charlottesville began demolishing the Vinegar Hill neighborhood in 1965. The city, however, deferred the most aggressive redevelopment of its new blank canvas to generations that followed in the 1980s. Separated by a span of fifteen years, future city leaders often did not connect the growth of the downtown and the creation of what we know today as the downtown mall to a racist urban renewal scheme. The passage of time, in other words, helped them achieve moral distance between what happened in the past and this new era in city development. In 2011, after decades of pressure, the city finally recognized its actions, and the city council delivered a public apology for the destruction of Vinegar Hill:

> Now therefore be it resolved that we, the undersigned members of the Charlottesville City Council recognize the African-American owned businesses, homes and property that were

destroyed or damaged by the razing of Vinegar Hill; acknowledge that the events leading to the destruction of this neighborhood did not adequately include those who were to be affected; mourn the lost sense of community caused by the demolition of this neighborhood; and for the harm caused we do hereby apologize for the City government's role in the destruction of the Vinegar Hill Neighborhood, and affirm the lessons learned from the City's actions will be remembered.

Today, the memory of Vinegar Hill, both what it was and how it was taken away, is at the center of many restorative projects. There's the New Hill Development Corporation, for example, that intends to build resources for "financial empowerment" with Charlottesville's Black community. The city itself has plans to incorporate Vinegar Hill more explicitly as part of the downtown's history through on-site plaques, markers, and memorials. At the Jefferson School, there's now a project underway, led by local resident Jordy Yager, to physically map inequality in Charlottesville by georeferencing property records. Projects like these are intended to keep structural inequality front and center as the modern city develops plans for affordable housing, negotiates with private developers, and determines what services it should fund or cut.

When I find myself near the statue of Robert E. Lee now, I am forced to concede that the physical world that white leaders of the past hoped would endure in fact did. Practice and research has taught me to sense the absence of the Black neighborhood that once stood not far from the spot, and nothing more than observation is required to see what replaced it: restaurants, retail, and pedestrian space that caters primarily to an upscale, white clientele. A city once ordered to preserve white racial purity is not so easily unordered.

Beliefs about racial purity in Virginia functioned like a Newton's cradle. Ideas became the spheres. Lift up the sphere that contains *What We Want to Believe* and send it crashing down. Kinetic energy lifts the sphere that contains *What We Fear*. Back and forth though these collisions, momentum is ongoing. All the power is saved. It has no end. If the science is sound it can continue forever, shockwave after shockwave after shockwave.

In August 2017, white supremacists who had organized through the Unite the Right campaign gathered once again at their shrines in Charlottesville, including Thomas Jefferson's University of Virginia. They were demonstrating violent power for their own pleasure but also, much like their predecessors in 1924, seeking to make their connections with the past explicit.

Many people were perplexed by the group's fixation on Charlottesville. There was, of course, ongoing controversy over the city's two Confederate statues and their potential removal from public space. Hate groups that converged on Charlottesville throughout that summer were using the monuments as convenient shorthand for what they felt was their wider entitlement—a world ordered and marked by white power. This explanation was understandable, but also not entirely satisfying. After all, New Orleans had removed its statues three months earlier, and while there were protests and agitation, the city had not been swarmed.

Maybe it was the Trump administration, the way his presidency and party had emboldened white supremacists? Hadn't Iowa Republican Steve King, like a Madison Grant impersonator, been tweeting bullshit that past spring about how "we can't restore our civilization with someone else's babies?" Wasn't Stephen Miller, one of Trump's key political advisors, also trapped in some armpit of ideas that hadn't been washed since 1924?

Perhaps there were even deeper and more clandestine forces at work in the white nationalist world, some power struggle within or among groups vying for dominant positions and claimed geographies. The rally's primary organizer, Jason Kessler, was a Charlottesville resident and a graduate of the University of Virginia. He had obvious ambitions toward securing an elevated place for himself among his fellow white supremacists.

As far as explaining why Unite the Right gathered in Charlottesville, none of these suggestions were wrong. They were just incomplete. That incompleteness became a void nervously filled with a familiar refrain: "This is not who we are," many people in Charlottesville said. "Our city will not tolerate division."

For others, however, the white nationalist rallies were a more combustible version of what the city had long been. Charlottesville was a finely articulated white space moving through time, impinging upon Black lives, first with enslavement and violence, then through residential segregation, statues, and racial integrity laws. Eventually, a backlash to civil rights bled into urban renewal. Now, it seemed, the city had settled upon an intentional strategy of finding itself powerless in the face of the status quo. In 2005, for example, long-serving city councilor Kathy Galvin, then a member of the city's school board, responded to a report about racial inequality in the city's school systems:

> The educational system is in and of itself neutral, even passive. White parents make it work for them through persistence and volunteer efforts. Black parents on the other hand expect the schools to work for them. . . . As a result, white kids learn to

prepare for college due to their parents' advocacy and black kids are left in the lurch due to their parents' lack of knowledge or experience with a good education.

The city also sometimes felt like a hostage to wealth and private development. Why could the city find ways to build homes for wealthy people but not everyone else? City planner Brian Haluska explained, "People complain that we're building 'housing for millionaires' but those [wealthier] people don't just go away. Instead, they'll outbid lower-income people on a $400,000 house and put a $300,000 addition on it." In Charlottesville, a lower-income homebuyer is now considered someone who lives in a $400,000 house. The University of Virginia, now turning a corner with new projects involving its history of enslavement and material improvements for non-faculty staff, is still one of the city's largest landowners, both as a public entity and as a private foundation.

On one hand, to say "This is not who we are" claims a truth that the days of mob rule and indiscriminate violence have passed. On the other, it denies the truth that other forms of acceptable destabilization have also worked to deny others their rightful legitimacy.

These competing claims were front and center in Charlottesville's November 2017 election. Even before the violence that summer, the campaign of community organizer Nikuyah Walker centered a promise to "unmask the illusion" of Charlottesville. To NPR, she referenced long-standing, unaddressed racial disparities and the unequal lives of lower-income residents. She explained, "The illusion [is] that we are a town everybody can thrive in."

The city's past leaders had often favored diluting these realities by aggressively employing aspirational narratives, the illusions that Walker referenced, that Charlottesville was a progressive, liberal enclave. Leaders seemed to hope that what the city could or would not deliver in urgent, material improvements, it made up for with good intentions. This diversion is common to politics generally, but there is something uniquely local about it is as well. The city of Thomas Jefferson's "academical village" could never be rotten from the inside. For Walker, and for the people who supported her campaign, it was not enough to name problems and propose solutions. The success of any proposal, her campaign implied, needed to be built on a foundation of honest and overdue reckoning about race and class.

In November, Walker secured the most votes in the city council race, and so became the first Black woman to become mayor in Charlottesville. It is tempting to wrap this detail into a narrative of progress, to hammer home that this story begins on a balmy day in 1924 when the Confederate statues were new, and that it ends with this cold November moment when the city regained its momentum on election night from attacks that radiated out from those same monuments. I could take advantage of the obvious here and tell you that the architects of Virginia's racial integrity laws would certainly find Walker's election a distressing turn of events.

But I want to end on a more ordinary moment. First, I should explain that in Charlottesville, "ordinary" has different meanings now. Today it is an ordinary thing, for example, to plan for the return of white supremacist violence. But it is also ordinary to be deeply motivated to take care of other residents. This care takes many forms. One involves a more truthful telling of the city's past, a secondary and often forgotten focus of a group of residents who assumed the responsibility of deliberating the fate of its Confederate statues. This body, the city's Blue Ribbon Commission on Race, Memorials, and Public Spaces, once said this responsibility involves breaking "the chain of racist transmission," challenging convictions about the past that work to conceal injustice. The statues, for example, were born of deeply racist origins. Clinging to narratives of their placement that frame them as benign honors has helped conceal this fact.

Now, even though the statues remain, it is an ordinary thing to find and enjoy evidence of this truth-telling in public space. Some efforts are anonymous. When the *New York Times* released its "1619 Project," a collective work attuned to the four-hundred-year anniversary of the arrival of America's first enslaved Africans, simple chalk graffiti around the city, red-numbered 1619s, called back to it. Flowers often appear at the small plaque that marks the spot of Charlottesville's slave auction block. Sometimes the word "slaves" is crossed out and improved in chalk so that the rewritten text reads: "On this site human beings were bought and sold."

One of the most sustained challenges to the illusory narratives is not anonymous at all, but a well-attended downtown walking tour conceptualized by Jalane Schmidt and Andrea Douglas, two Black historians. The tour, which is free, uses monuments and downtown geography to branch into deeper conversations about race, space, and the city's past. Last summer, just as the historians were concluding one of their tours, I passed through the park where the statue of Robert E. Lee sits. It was an ordinary day, which means the city was on high alert for acts of violence; on this occasion it was even more so because the second anniversary of the 2017 attacks was days away.

The statue of Lee, which most often acts as a cold voyeur of the lives of unhoused people and downtown workers, sits in a tiny park. Its closest neighbors are the main branch of the Charlottesville library, where my partner works, and the Albemarle Charlottesville Historical Society. When I moved to the area, local historians explained to me that the downtown historical society had a reputation for being the white historical society, positioning itself in ways—both subtle and not-so-subtle—against the Jefferson School, the community's African American heritage center.

It didn't take long to understand what they meant. The historical society's presence was conspicuously absent in the city's public programming about its Confederate monuments. It was also obstructive in the attempts historians and reporters made to find out information about the provenance of Klan paraphernalia in its collections. "I think it's fair to say things have changed," former director Stephen Meeks told the press. I have never understood if he was suggesting that we were in a more enlightened era, and therefore didn't need to trouble ourselves with things he felt it was best for us not to know, or if he was complaining about the new terms on which the community wanted to know about its past. In July 2019, when the city commemorated the life of lynching victim John Henry James, a Black ice cream vendor killed by a white mob in 1898, Meeks's replacement used the occasion and his personal Facebook page to remind people that white people were lynched too.

That day, things were relatively quiet in the park despite the looming anniversary. I was not there to linger. I was simply trying to get from one place to the next. But then, coming past the library, I saw police snipers on the roof of the historical society, where they had staked out a vantage point to monitor the park below. Later, I learned that the people who had attended the walking tour had also noticed their presence. In the two years since the attacks, heavy surveillance is a new form of daily violence, which the city feels is an acceptable trade-off in preventing larger threats to public order.

The historical society wanted to be helpful to the police, and perhaps felt it could not refuse their request. Objectively, I can acknowledge that. But here is what I saw: from atop it, agents of the state pointed guns below at a public attempting to break the racist chain of transmission, members of the same public that had attempted and failed to enlist the historical society in their prior efforts.

The city leaders who celebrated the placement of Lee's statue in 1924 promised that everyone who came to that spot would receive the lessons of the past. "To teach" can also mean to make someone suffer to an extent so great that it has a conditioning effect—*That will teach you a lesson*. By the consequence of their mortality, these leaders deferred the pleasure of instruction to their statue, unliving but no less rooted in what they hoped would be a lasting articulation of their power. Attempts to make this power endure can look like repressive laws, failed science, and combustible violence. But it can also feel like a gun pointed at you on an ordinary day. And sometimes that's exactly what it is.

CHAPTER THREE:

HEALING LANDSCAPES

I n 1934, Joseph DeJarnette, the superintendent of Western State Hospital in Staunton, Virginia, made an excursion to the nearby mountains that, on any other morning, he might only have seen as distant, blue-hazed peaks from the window of his office. Western State had been constructed to maximize opportunities for its patients to view Virginia's Blue Ridge, and DeJarnette's predecessors believed the mountain landscape was therapeutic, scenery able to calm a troubled mind. On this trip in 1934, however, the mountains did not calm DeJarnette at all. Quite the opposite.

"Last December it was my experience to visit a mountainous section of our own beloved Virginia," he wrote in his 1935 superintendent's report of his trip the previous year, "where I found one family numbering 16 children, 12 of whom I saw, and at a glance could grade their mentality as imbeciles." He continued, "This family was living in the direst poverty without any of the decencies and comforts of life. I was told there were 50 other families living in the same county under similar environment and with the same degree of mentality. What does this mean?"

Fear not, because DeJarnette told us:

> It means that Virginia is allowing to accumulate within her borders hordes of these clans who have no right to be born, who are challenging the intelligence of her citizenry, who are furnishing her courts with crime and criminals, and who are

placing on her treasury incalculable burdens.

Of course he tried to calculate the exact amount of that burden.

"If this one family which I visited is allowed to propagate in six generations it will dethrone the Jukes and the Kallikak families," he wrote, referencing often-cited cacogenic families that had become classic eugenic boogeymen. These successive generations, DeJarnette argued, would "add millions of dollars in relief work and an endless trail of social sores wherever they settle." But, he promised, "welfare workers are cooperating with us in an effort to sterilize the whole family."

Almost a decade after the publication of *Mongrel Virginians* and the passage of Virginia's Sterilization and Racial Integrity Acts, the mountains remained a crucible of progress for the state's eugenicists. They could not admit defeat, of course, or concede in some rare moment of rationality that their math did not make sense. If their plans were working, if their logic was sound, then why was the number of "defectives" growing?

DeJarnette concluded his report from the mountains by sharing a favorite quote of his from William "Dean" Inge, an influential English eugenicist and Anglican priest: "The State has as good a right to remove undesirable citizens as a gardener has to weed his garden." Knowing nothing about English gardening myself, I might ask: Is it more acceptable in England for a gardener to toil ten years in the same plot of land, never improving it, and only succeeding in dirtying his hands?

Here might be an even stranger question: How does one weed a mountain?

Unfortunately, Virginia has an answer for that question too.

Shenandoah National Park, located in Virginia's Blue Ridge Mountains, is currently one of the most reliable drivers of tourism for eight central Virginia counties, including mine. A recent economic impact study conducted by the park and released in June 2019 notes that in the previous year, the park's 1.26 million visitors had "a cumulative benefit to the local economy of $116 million." The lion's share of that benefit, an impressive $87 million, came directly from visitor spending.

Today, the official line from the National Park Service is that the robust economic impact of its parks is a happy bonus. Jeffrey Olson, its chief of communications, recently told NPR's *Marketplace*, "National Parks were not created to be the economic contributors that they are. They were created to preserve and protect these wonderful, natural, historic and cultural landscapes of the country. It just so happens that . . . there's also this economic value that [park visitors] leave behind in the communities they visit."

This is a pleasing idea that hits the right notes—that good was done and that passive, tremendous profits followed. But I tend to believe that Shenandoah National Park *was* created with both private and public profits in mind. I also tend to believe that eugenics played a part in making that profit possible.

In Virginia, the eugenics movement bestowed a broad freedom to the powerful to articulate, and then act on, their ideas about the concessions so-called unproductive citizens owed to the state. The state felt that a great number of people fit the description of "unproductive" and therefore owed the government their reproductive freedom—taking something from an individual would make things better for the whole. Four years after the Sterilization and Racial Integrity Acts were passed, a similar logic of taking and giving found its way into the creation of the Shenandoah National Park, which was aided by a sweeping eminent domain law Virginia produced in 1928.

When people say that something was created for the public good, the part of my brain that still fully operates as a historian asks, "But what did 'public good' mean back then?

And who claimed the authority to set its definition?" And in the case of Shenandoah, these questions are very material in understanding how this asset came to be.

In creating the park, both the state and federal government had to determine the fate of mountain settlements that existed within what would be the new park's boundaries. Couldn't the people living in the mountains just continue to live there? Sure, but the park's developers didn't like that because many of those people were poor. The things the residents wanted and needed to do to the land were not compatible with the principles of conservation—one definition of "public good"— that the government wanted to carry forward. The mountain folks would farm, raise livestock, hunt, and fish. They would cut down trees and burn wood. They might also freak out tourists. *Here comes the Smith family down from Richmond out on their weekend hike and, oh no, it's a group of hillbillies ahead . . .*

To manage this dilemma, the government decided to displace the mountain people, some five hundred or so families, using its newly acquired powers of eminent domain. In other words, harm done to a smaller number of individuals would be balanced by the creation of an asset that would benefit the whole. There is enough grief attached to that element alone in this story, but the government also opened a kind of Pandora's box with its actions. In attempting to justify its decisions, a range of powerful people cast mountain families in the role of defective citizens, glorified squatters on valuable land. Once labeled like this, they could not be unlabeled. Bureaucracies that later had a hand in determining what came next for them used these labels too. And for some of the people in these mountain settlements, what came next were institutions like the Lynchburg Colony and Western State.

Because I grew up near the Smoky Mountains in East Tennessee, I am assuming some personal risk by admitting that the landscapes of Virginia's Blue Ridge Mountains and the Shenandoah Valley are the most beautiful I have ever seen. DeJarnette's predecessors happened to be right, I think. The landscape has therapeutic qualities, a way of enveloping onlookers in calming panoramas of sky and mountain without end.

Both regions yield varied terrain, but the Tennessee Smokies are a little less generous to tourists who aren't practiced outdoor enthusiasts. There, waterfalls and vistas, spring blooms and fall leaves become more precious as the ruggedness of mountain land increases. The Blue Ridge Mountains in Virginia, in contrast, offer gentler points of access. One of the great pleasures of these mountains comes from just gazing upon them, with no exploration required.

My assessment also happens to track with several of the reasons behind the government's decision to locate its first southern national park in Virginia, rather than in Tennessee (although that was on the horizon, and yes, there is a displacement story to tell there as well). But by 1925, the selection committee working on the decision had concluded, "the Great Smokies have some handicaps which will make the development of them into a national park a matter of delay; their very ruggedness and height make road and other park development a serious undertaking as to time and expense."

Tennessee's loss became Virginia's gain. A new national park meant recreation and conservation, but community boosters in Virginia didn't need to be in complete harmony with these aims to understand other benefits the park might bring as well. Its development meant the federal government would help build infrastructure, like roads that would bring visitors and their automobiles, as well all the tourist dollars that would come with them.

The new national park would also help business leaders in the Shenandoah Valley settle a score with the urban parts of the state. Nationally, the United States became "urban" in the 1920s, meaning that more people were living in cities than in rural areas for the first time. But this transition came more slowly to places like Virginia, and it produced familiar tensions between rural and urban populations. These tensions could be practical, like debates about how state funding should be allocated, or ideological, like the often-litigated question of who the "real" Americans are. Virginia remained a predominately rural state until the 1950s, but local leaders in the Valley anticipated their eventual demotion to the role of dead weight as cities continued to siphon up state resources and migrants from the countryside.

But with a solid economy, new roads, and flourishing businesses, all courtesy of the park—*people from the North spending their money down here for a change*—the best and brightest might not always leave for greener pastures. Even more might settle that part of the state. Local supporters pledged to honor "a new spirit to boost, to advertise, to seek new settlers, to invite tourists and above all to unite and co-operate to win for the Shenandoah Valley her just place in The Sun."

Wilderness entrepreneur George Freeman Pollock embodied this ambition and became a booster like no other. In the 1890s, he had settled in the Shenandoah Valley in an attempt to make good on a doomed inheritance. His late father had been the principal owner of a failed copper mine and his debt included just over 5,000 heavily mortgaged Blue Ridge acres. Pollock attempted to redeem the investment by transforming the acreage into a recreation area, which he called Skyland Resort, for well-heeled outdoorsmen from northern Virginia, Maryland, Washington, DC, and New York. As momentum for the national park was building, he positioned himself as a trusted advisor to park planners, an insider who could work in the service of outsiders.

There is no doubt Pollock loved the mountains. But he had considerably less esteem for his mountain neighbors. Park historian Darwin Lambert wrote, "to avoid being driven from the Blue Ridge, [Pollock] dominated the mountain folk, sometimes with a gun, sometimes by understanding their motives better than they did, sometimes by sheer nerve." But Pollock used another form of domination as well. Eventually, he helped attract academic interest in his neighbors' genetic fitness. The research that followed was used to assess the "needs" of mountaineers during the great transformation of the inhabited land into a national park.

I will call Pollock a grifter because I can think of no better term to describe the way he executed his ambitions. By 1925, he believed he was the owner of a mountain empire like none other. And standing at the center of this empire was the rustic luxury of his Skyland Resort. While he claimed to possess what he hoped would be the future park's most prized land, however, Pollock was actually in debt for much of his life. His well-connected patrons and resort guests often helped bail him out of his more urgent financial crises. "I am afraid I would have lost my hold on the mountain if it had not been for Mr. Byrd," Pollock wrote, referring to Virginia Senator Harry F. Byrd. "And if I had lost my hold on the mountain, there would have been no Shenandoah National Park." Clearly, this was not a humble man.

Even those who knew Pollock in his twilight years considered him an impressive businessman, despite convincing evidence to the contrary. "Pollock's ability in business must have been substantial," Lambert muses. "How else could he, starting without firmly tangible assets, continually improve and expand his complex enterprise?" He then offers a disclaimer: "But he operated at a financial loss and was seldom if ever out of debt." Pollock's supporters reconciled these attributes by embracing him as a man whose generosity was his own worst enemy.

Besides, what's a little debt when there's a good time to show for it? Pollock preserved the tales of his own exploits in a camp newsletter called the *Stony Man Camp Bugle Call*, which had around 200 subscribers who wanted the latest mountain gossip about the season's cake walks, theatrical performances, dances, minstrel shows, and, in August 1901, even an elaborate jousting tournament. "Mr. Pollock rode as Knight of Skyland, riding for Miss Willie Stealy with purple and white colors." one article reported. "The knights were all dressed in armor, the suits being very handsome with breastplates of silver and silver helmets, with boots and leggings." Who can put a price on that kind of fun?

If Pollock's elaborate wilderness parties were achieved at the expense of missed tax or mortgage payments, it could be easy to think of him, as his supporters did, as a charming eccentric. But he could certainly be a ruthless businessman when the occasion called for it, and this happened often in his dealings with his mountain neighbors.

Pollock regarded many of his neighbors as nothing more than squatters, hillbillies who had plopped themselves down in crags and crannies without any respect for the concept of legal ownership. In his memoir, *Skyland: Heart of the Shenandoah National Park*, he writes that upon the death of his father, he followed the family lawyer's instructions to immediately make a settlement in the mountains by fencing in 125 acres as his home base. Naturally, lawyers would sort out any title complications, but in the meantime, he could defend his land with force if necessary. Without a sense of irony that his strategy involved claiming and occupying land with no legal right of ownership—exactly what squatters do—Pollock became a mountaineer.

His title complications proved to be more complex than he anticipated due to his large mortgage debt and his own lack of capital. But in Pollock's world, even his creditors found him charming. He had a bizarre habit of dressing up as Teddy Roosevelt when the nature of his business required him to travel to Charlottesville to plead for an extension on his debt payments:

> During these years . . . I adopted a costume copied from pictures of the costume worn by Teddy Roosevelt in the West—corduroy trousers with high boots and a corduroy hunting shirt, which came down over the trousers nearly to the knees, elaborately trimmed with leather fringe. The outer edge of the trousers was trimmed likewise. I wore a regular U. S. Army canvas belt with a .45-calibre Colt revolver strapped around my waist and a ten-gallon hat. . . . I always wore my cowboy outfit, and the Judge would listen and smile a little and always give me more time. God bless him!

On the mountain, one family in particular, the Nicholsons, seemed to bear the brunt of Pollock's sense of entitlement about his questionable ownership of mountain land. Pollock often described patriarch Aaron Nicholson as "the king of squatters in the region." He insisted that Aaron's claim of ownership was made on nothing more than a doddering old man's understanding of how the world should work, that because Aaron had cleared that land, built homes upon it, and farmed it, then it was his and not Pollock's. Pollock, of course, disagreed. "My father and Mr. Allen [his father's former business partner] owned most of the land upon which they [the Nicholson family] were living," he writes of his inheritance.

The Potomac Appalachian Trail Club, whose wealthy members frequently visited Pollock's resort, even memorialized Aaron Nicholson in a cartoon printed on souvenir maps of the area. Rendering him as "The King of Free State Hollow," the exaggerated mountain man, barefoot and toting a gun, says, "It's all my land . . . I surweyed it - chopped 'round it myself - from Peak to Peak as fur as I can see."

Pollock, in his memoir, claims Nicholson shouted those lines at surveyors who had come to examine the land. At that time Pollock was embroiled in what he considered to be a nuisance legal action with a third party who was angling to determine how much land he actually owned so that it might be seized as an asset for unpaid debts. Hoping to get rid of the surveyors, Pollock's story goes, he routed them down to Nicholson's farm, telling them to ask Nicholson who owned the land. The joke is that Pollock knew, at least in this tall tale, that Nicholson would threaten the surveyors in typical hillbilly fashion by treating them to the business end of a shotgun and an incoherent lecture about squatter's rights. According to Pollock, the plan worked beautifully. The surveyors fled, never to return. "And so I could go on, with story after story of the miraculous escapes I had while I struggled along to get my title," he writes, desperate to add a sense of adventure to what are, without his exaggerations, simply tales of dodging taxes and borrowing money from wealthy friends.

The postscript to that story is that an archaeological team led by Audrey Horning later discovered, in surveys conducted on behalf of the Park Service in the late-1990s, that Aaron Nicholson did indeed own at least 241 acres of land.

In his own estimation, Pollock was, as he described himself, "a small wart, if you please, on the nose of a beautiful woman," an annoying fixture marring a pleasant view and surprisingly difficult to remove.

In February 1925, the *Page News and Courier*, the local paper for Luray, Virginia, printed a letter from Pollock. He composed it at his winter retreat in New York, but it was intended for his summer neighbors down south.

He urged the mountaineers:

> By all means sell your holdings to the Government and apply for work just as soon as improvements within the Park begin; you will get good pay near home; you probably will not have to leave the farm which you sold to the government, the old folks can continue to raise the little crops, your growing children will soon have schools to attend, and if you are careful with what you earn, you will soon save up enough money to buy a place elsewhere, if you desire it.

He promised them, "you will have a good deal provided for you by Uncle Sam."

But that was all speculation. Although President Coolidge authorized the Shenandoah National Park in May 1925, the act left the precise boundaries of the future park, and a strategy for acquiring the land, to be determined. The only thing certain was that the federal government wouldn't be purchasing the land, and it would not deal with anyone who claimed title to it directly. If Virginia wanted this enterprise, Virginia would pay for it and donate the landholdings to the federal government.

State leaders, along with some of their Washington allies, had predicted this scenario, and as a show of good faith, they had spent the previous year engaged in elaborate fundraising campaigns. Contributors were offered the opportunity to symbolically buy acreage in the new park (Pollock "bought" one thousand acres, which translated to a pledge of around $6,000). Politicians campaigned for the park on the promise that it would bring enormous wealth to the area in the form of tourist revenue, as well as an influx of a better class of in-migrants, who would be charmed by the state's beauty and entrepreneurial spirit.

This coordinated campaign was no joke. William E. Carson, Virginia's newly appointed chairman of conservation, praised the state's fundraising activity with some wonder:

> pledges from the people were taken in amounts running from six to twenty thousand dollars and when we analyzed the campaign we found that little or no information was at hand as to the extent of the area, as to the value of the land within the area, as to the condition of the titles of the land, as to whether the people wanted to sell their lands, nor was there any definite assurance that the United States Government would accept it, and yet the idea was sold, the area in which it was to be established named, and approximately twenty-six thousand pledges secured.

This sort of single-minded determination might have seemed alien to me had I not lived through 2018, another moment in which the powerful tried to call forth a similar kind of new era in Virginia. That was the year of the Amazon HQ2 pitch competition and the successful bid by representatives of Alexandria and Arlington, Virginia. Pitch season taught us a lot about how much localities were willing to give up for a chance at business. In Virginia's case, it was a minimum of $750 million in cash incentives that would be traded for the potential to attract better talent, boost job numbers, and earn Amazon's gratitude. From my vantage point, forging this relationship required unfathomable levels of politicking and boosterism that were cloaked in the outward projection of a message that all Virginians shared our leaders' great enthusiasm for the opportunity. Governor Ralph Northam, in all our names, turned the state motto into an instance of corporate branding and proclaimed, "Virginia is for Amazon Lovers."

This might be a crass comparison to make in the context of an asset that, almost a century removed from the events I'm describing, is deeply beloved. But it helps to underscore the fact that before the Shenandoah National Park was a place, it was a pitch, executed through pamphlets exclaiming "EVERYBODY WANTS IT" that were disseminated by politically appointed negotiators who referred to themselves as leaders of a war party. And the most nonnegotiable element of this pitch was its central incentive: free and clear title to an enormous tract of land, without encumbrances or monies owed, gifted to the federal government.

The initial goal was the acquisition of 385,500 acres. Virginia appointed Chairman Carson to oversee the process. Throughout 1926 and 1927, the state continued fundraising while it sent engineers to the Shenandoah Valley to perform land and title assessments. They returned with discouraging results. The first mass survey indicated that their target included 5,650 individual parcels, on which sat 3,250 homes occupied by at least 7,000 people. Katrina Powell, an English professor at Virginia Tech who has written about the displacement of mountain families during the park's creation, found that park boosters intentionally misrepresented the size of the local population during early planning. That included Pollock, who assured the government they would find only "a few small mountain farms, of no great value." That there was a significant difference between the anticipated and actual number of inhabitants was not an expected discovery.

The National Park Service ordered a resurvey, and on the basis of that, it reduced the park's size to 327,000 acres. It would reduce it again, to around 160,000 acres, before the park eventually opened. The state agreed to appropriate at least a million dollars for land purchases, and a number of large donors in the Rockefeller and Carnegie stratosphere came on board. Chairman Carson hated the work. "To boot-lick a lot of rich men is a job that doesn't suit a man of my kidney," he wrote to his friend Harry Byrd.

In 1928, Virginia helped lessen that boot-licking burden by passing the Public Park Condemnation Act, which granted the state authority to secure park land through eminent domain. It was one thing to fundraise or appropriate a target sum, but quite another to leverage that sum in the actual acquisition of land. There were, of course, landowners who didn't need to be coerced to sell, but state officials encountered a variety of obstacles. It was often difficult to make contact with owners, disputes arose about the price of land, some landowners refused to sell, and surveys ignited conflicting claims of ownership. A worrisome number of tenant farmers had also been left in limbo; having no right to be compensated, they were at the mercy of the state's actions.

"It was manifestly hopeless to undertake to acquire the necessary area by direct purchase," Carson reported, "in which any of the thousands of owners or claimants could hold up the entire project unless paid exorbitant and unfair prices, with jury trials, appeals, and all the endless delays which can be injected into ordinary proceedings by selfish, stubborn and avaricious litigants." It was left unsaid that the exorbitant prices seemed to be the state's own fundraising figure—five or six dollars per acre—which the state now felt was a mercenary amount, evidence that mountain people intended to be greedy.

Although the park continued to enjoy enormous support among local business leaders, phrases like "park propaganda" began appearing in the local press and in the letters concerned residents sent to state and federal officials. One of the wealthier landowners filed an ultimately unsuccessful suit for an injunction to stop land condemnation. The condemnation law would uncomplicate the bureaucratic machinery that was straining toward the new national park. But for some, it made the state appear cruel at worst and wasteful at best. If the land was so valuable, some citizens argued, why give it to the federal government? In classic Virginia fashion, a professor at UVA ignited a small campaign to abandon the national park in favor of a state park, which, in his reasoning, could at least be segregated according to state law, sparing white tourists the indignity of race-mixing. Lewis Willis, a landowner from Marys Rock, summed up the misery of waiting to have his land seized by the state in a 1932 letter to President Hoover:

> The national park was conceived in ambition, brought forth by an appeal to greed, and fed on exaggerations and misstatements. . . . We are willing to make any reasonable sacrifice for the public good when necessary. We are unwilling to part with our homes to advertise a few politicians and to help a small part of our population get their hands into tourists' pockets.

By studying letters sent by mountain families to the government during displacement, Katrina Powell concludes that it was difficult for landowners to challenge or resist the condemnation process, largely because of misinformation, some unintentional and some not, about the project. Pollock, in his role as park promoter, for example, spread word through local newspapers that "Uncle Sam" intended to let many families remain on their land as tenants for the foreseeable future, and that the more spry mountaineers would be well-placed to come aboard the park project as paid workers, clearing the land and helping build infrastructure. I am speculating here, but I find it likely that Pollock actually believed that the most compliant mountaineers might "earn" their right to remain by offering some service to their government, even if it was only their public gratitude.

This is what all grifters believe, isn't it? That reinvention comes easily to the ambitious. "Cons thrive in times of transition and fast change," argues psychologist Maria Konnikova in *The Confidence Game*, and I nod, knowing what comes next in this story.

Much like the state, Pollock was prepared to tax the limits of his own resources to ensure the best outcome for the future park. Skyland Resort became the de facto headquarters of that enterprise, and Pollock treated park planners to fine dining, illegal alcohol, and a range of entertainments. He wrote letters to local papers, attended community meetings, and continually took on duties as a tour guide. He set out to impress and persuade and was immensely successful in this regard.

During the initial phases of park planning, Pollock often made it a point to take his visitors through the homesteads of his poorest neighbors, mixing colorful tales of mountain life with scenery that was intended to cultivate the same attitude of paternalism that he harbored toward these families himself. "I knew that without actually visiting these people in their homes," Pollock wrote, describing one trip in his memoir, "one could never conceive of their poverty and wretchedness." These trips, by and large, were intended to soothe the hearts and minds of park promoters who had the prospect of the mountain residents' displacement weighing on them. Pollock seemed to understand that a powerful corrective to their hesitation could come by reframing displacement as a gain rather than a loss. Instead of being villains, park promoters could be the heroes who saved the mountain people from their own worst impulses by coaxing them toward a more civilized life.

What Pollock undoubtedly left out of these tales is that he had a hand in making that poverty. Many of his neighbors, by choice or from a lack of other options, were part of his enterprise and worked directly at Skyland Resort or played some role in its economy by supplying labor for its construction projects or the goods its guests consumed. "Those of Corbin Hollow depended on us for their livelihood," Pollock wrote, framing the residents' employment as a kind of charitable arrangement. He was even prone to attributing his sorry financial state to his employees. "In the fall of the year," he complained, "poor Pollock had nothing left except the improvements which had been made to Skyland and its surroundings."

The payments Pollock made for various services could come in the form of cash or, when things were tight, in unwanted shit lying around Skyland, including records, books, clothing left by guests, or damaged china and crockery. In Corbin Hollow, for example, archaeologists working in 1995 found a dumping pile that contained at least thirty-eight pairs of dress shoes in good condition, suggesting that the things Pollock sometimes offered in lieu of payment had little utility for his employees.

But that was just the way things were in that part of the mountain, and some residents found a way to make it work for them when they could. Playing the part of the hillbilly for rich tourists could help mountaineers sell moonshine or handcrafts, for example. Taking their chances with Pollock might have appeared to be a safer bet than relocation. The same archaeological team also found that "the presence of Skyland certainly kept residents in the hollow when the natural increase and the division of lands would have ordinarily encouraged out-migration."

Writing much earlier, Darwin Lambert came to similar conclusions.

> The people did not know they were "mountaineers" until outsiders convinced them that they were. Pollock and his guests, romanticizing them in that way as far back as the 1890s—using them as entertainers and mysterious dangers, servants and laborers, sources of liquor and objects of charity— convinced those of the Skyland section and made a lot of them dependents, holding in the mountains many who would have otherwise left. It was in the Skyland vicinity that NPS officials and others formed their early, largely adverse view of the people.

This adverse view helped park promoters reason that the mountain residents would benefit from a sudden and icy plunge into the modern world. Wage work would be better than subsistence living, and the more ambitious and capable mountaineers might seek opportunities that grew out of the region's new tourist economy. Park planners did not entertain the idea that some mountaineers were already part of a tourist economy and that their fortunes had not risen. They preferred to think of mountaineers as mild and complacent people who needed a helpful push toward the twentieth century.

It is easy to imagine the Blue Ridge Mountains as pastoral and rural, peppered with small village communities and subsistence farms, not to mention George Pollock's famous retreat. But let us imagine it another way: as a place just thirty miles from the University of Virginia and two hours from the nation's capital, where visitors from Washington, both tourists and individuals attached to the park project, regularly encountered mountaineers. On one hand, it became a common but incorrect trope that these mountain families knew little of the outside world. But on the other, it was certain that the outside world knew about them.

In 1928, the same year Virginia authorized the Public Park Condemnation Act, a young educator named Miriam Sizer, a recent graduate of the University of Virginia, moved to the Blue Ridge. Her first patron was George Pollock, who secured and funded employment for her at a summer school that had been established for mountain residents. I do not know the original terms between Sizer and Pollock, but it is clear that within two months of her arrival, she had positioned herself, by choice or encouragement, but likely a combination of both, as a researcher rather than a teacher.

She was introduced to senior park officials by Pollock, who had sent the secretary of the interior an essay Sizer had written and that she was intending to submit to the *New York Times*. In her letter of introduction to John Bohn of the *Times*, she indicated that "at Mr. Pollock's suggestion," she had made a study of the sociological conditions within the future park. She wrote, with a dramatic flourish, that the mountaineers were a "modern Robinson Crusoe, without his knowledge of civilization. Steeped in ignorance, wrapped in self-satisfaction and complacency, possessed of little or no ambition, little sense of citizenship, little comprehension of law, or respect for law, these people present a problem that demands and challenges the attention of thinking men and women."

When I read Sizer's letter, I imagine her boldly adding "and women" to the end of a dispatch she hoped would impress an editor at the *Times*. This is often what eugenics looked like as well—just someone trying to advance their own interests, making their life bigger as others' became smaller.

Sizer believed, as she explained to the *Times* and in later correspondence, that the government had a responsibility to mountain families beyond paying them for land that was needed for park development. Without an intervening hand, she stressed, a good many of the mountaineers would become paupers and criminals, spreading their taste for liquor and love of gambling, their loose morals and lawlessness, to cities and towns. In her assessment, it would be better for the government to *do something* with them. Sizer, like Pollock, believed she had an important part to play in what was to come. She first imagined something like a reservation for the poorest families. It would provide a place where they could go, but it could also manage them with a corrective, containing influence.

As Sizer's ideas developed, many were not at all problematic on the surface. She was right that both the state and federal government had a responsibility to help the poor. She was also correct that simply chasing the residents off the land and into cities was not a sustainable plan, not least of all because the cities would not exactly be welcoming. She pointed out, at some personal risk presumably, that the closest localities were not doing the things they ought to do to prepare for displacement, like making sure their schools could accommodate an influx of new pupils.

But Sizer's ideas were also predicated on inflexible beliefs and professional training that led her to conclude that mountaineers were poorly developed physically and mentally and were incapable of engineering their own survival. She felt pity for them, but it was what it was.

At that time, federal and state officials did not have a coherent plan to deal with the enormity of displacement. In a worsening economy, even mountaineers who were able to secure payment for their land would have to go somewhere. And there would be no *Beverly Hillbillies* moment where families loaded their meager possessions onto trucks and rode off to better things. Pollock favored a system that would get rid of the worst people, but that would allow the better educated residents (along with the more "wizened up" older mountaineers, as he might call them) to remain in the park as laborers and tenants. After 1933, New Deal programs would also make additional options possible. But in the last years of the twenties, the subject of relocation was Virginia's burden alone.

Park officials were put off by Sizer immediately. I am not her biographer by any means, but in her correspondence, which is admittedly meager, she reads as the type of person who always wanted to show that she was the smartest person in the room, and that attitude likely played badly with struggling park planners. This was a delicate stage in the development of the national park. The agreement as it existed meant the federal government would not be involved in any arrangements about land or people in order to make the chain of custody as pure as possible. Wouldn't trying to resettle these people indicate the government had misgivings about those arrangements? William Carson had to clean up behind the scenes and rein Sizer in to assure the project's federal monitors that "the best thing that can be done for these people is to have the Government come in and take the land."

But other people who had an inkling of what was coming did take an interest in Sizer's work, likely finding out about it through Pollock and his network. In 1929, Mandel Sherman, the director of the recently established, Rockefeller-funded Washington Child Research Center, proposed a full academic investigation of the families living in the proposed park. For scientists like Sherman, who imagined geography as an impermeable boundary and the mountaineers as perfectly quarantined subjects, the mountains were a kind of laboratory offering tightly controlled conditions. Here were virgin, unstudied subjects not yet contaminated by the modern world or, perhaps most importantly, an association with other scholars. The relationship between nutrition, environment, personality, and intelligence could be studied, and Sherman, given his patron, was particularly interested in the impact of these forces on child development. A sociologist by training, Sherman partnered with a science writer from the *Washington Evening Star*, Thomas Henry, and invited Sizer to serve as a fieldworker on their research team.

What a moment this must have been for Sizer. Having used her initiative to advocate for the importance of her work and training, she had become, less than a year after her arrival in the mountains, a key player in an honest to god field study that promised to be of national importance. Of course, this meant she would remain in the mountains indefinitely so that Sherman and Henry could attach their names to data that she collected. But she would also be one of those "thinking women" that she had described so boldly in her letter to the *Times*.

In 1929, President Herbert Hoover decided to build a vacation home in the future park, which made the mountain children there a subject of national interest and came as something of a boon for Sherman's team. When Charles Lindbergh visited, the president discovered his neighbors didn't recognize the aviator, so he decided to fund a new mountain school along with a teacher-in-residence, Christine Vest. Sherman and Henry described the school's opening as a helpful base for researchers, who arrived "armed with form boards, pennies, chewing tobacco, stacks of intelligence tests, note books and other paraphernalia of the university psychological laboratory."

(And yes, I have been kept up at night, consumed by

the idea that Charles Lindbergh's hurt feelings at not being recognized might have somehow led to psychologists experimenting on rural children.)

Whatever might have compelled Sherman and Henry originally, researchers were excited at the possibility that the Blue Ridge might provide them with an opportunity to complicate (to use contemporary academic-speak) the nature versus nurture debate. For the researchers, a pattern emerged that was plain to see. The families living deep within the future park were the most troubled and impoverished, while those living closer to cities and towns fared better.

Of course, the researchers, who published their findings in a book called *Hollow Folk* in 1933, described the Blue Ridge families using hallmark eugenic language. Many of the mountaineers, for example, are described as having "pure stock" that was nonetheless in the process of deteriorating due to unhealthy environments and lifestyles. Eighty years later, incidentally, J. D. Vance would make a similar argument in the pages of *Hillbilly Elegy*, stating that people of good Scots-Irish stock took a wrong turn and let poverty take root in their bloodlines. *Hollow Folk* was also predicated on a eugenic axiom, that "because there has been only occasional mingling with people from other extractions," then the conclusions and findings about the intelligence and development of subjects were more credible.

Because the study was of interest to child development specialists, researchers also gave ample attention to matters like illegitimate births and the fertility of the poorest women. This put the researchers' work into what a genteel Virginia judge called "cordial sympathy" with other core ideas of the eugenics movement and race science. In one of the more chilling passages, researchers question if poor mountain women, who are thought to give birth without complaint, might be genetically predisposed to higher pain thresholds and if this reality might bear some relationship to their capacity for difficult, physical labor. This myth is borrowed directly from contemporary medical opinions about Black people and particularly Black women, which in turn originated from depraved ideas held by slaveowners. In 1851, Dr. Samuel Cartwright, in *Diseases and Peculiarities of the Negro Race*, argued that both enslaved workers and "free negroes" were susceptible to a disease called *dysaesthesia aethiopica*, a mental illness indistinguishable from laziness that also produced an insensitivity of the skin and nerves and could be cured by regular whipping.

As a historical document, *Hollow Folk* is useful for seeing these ideas in flux and tracking how a hardline emphasis on race and genetics could assume the softer bordering of cultural theories without changing the ultimate conclusions. This softer bordering is a strategy still employed by eugenicists today, who often claim a middle ground in the nature versus nature debate as long as they are able to reach conclusions that buttress their beliefs about the inarguable inferiority of certain classes, races, and groups. The long career of contemporary political scientist and white supremacist Charles Murray, for example, is a testament to the usefulness of this flexibility. After arguing, on the basis of IQ testing, that Black people are irreversibly less intelligent than white people in 1994's *The Bell Curve*, Murray has pivoted in recent years to the subject of white plight and the genetic realities of class structure.

Sherman and Henry were similarly interested in proving and tracking devolution, both genetic and cultural. They perhaps would have disagreed with some of their contemporaries about the extent to which it could be reversed, but the pattern was clear to them, and that is what excited them. The deeper one traveled within the future park, the closer one got to the rot.

Perhaps there was some truth to this, because another

reading of *Hollow Folk* is that the families facing the most severe hardships also just happened to be George Pollock's closest neighbors. That the presence of Skyland, tourists, and Pollock's economic control might have some bearing on the lives of mountain families is not considered by researchers to any significant degree. And yet, affirming signs appear casually in the text. In one passage, a man watching his wife give birth tells her not to act like a "hotel leydy" (Sherman and Henry sometimes tried to write in mountain dialect) by giving into the pain, instructions that presumably conveyed his expectation that his wife have a stronger constitution than city women.

One of the saddest descriptions of mountain life, for me, comes through a tableau of a moment in Corbin Hollow, the closest settlement to Skyland. Researchers find women in evening gowns while their young children are dressed in burlap. It's a situation the researchers describe as "curious" and nothing more, even though they presumably understand that the gowns are cast-offs from hotel guests. They are not concerned with exploring what it might be like to be a woman digging rotten vegetables out of the ground in an evening gown or why Pollock or his guests felt fancy, impractical clothing was an acceptable form of charity or even payment for services rendered.

In what we are told is the mountain's most isolated cabin, researchers discover an old mountaineer listening to phonographic records, a story that provides an odd segue to a discussion of primitive music. Again, it is obvious the phonograph and records are junk from Pollock's hotel, but there is no interest on the part of researchers to explain how they got there or what kind of intercommunity market might exist for goods and services. The researchers' only comment is that the mountaineer's favorite record is a murder ballad, "intensely realistic to him."

By the time *Hollow Folk* was published, residents of the Blue Ridge had inspired articles in a number of national papers, including the *New York Times* and the *Washington Post*. Henry had made them the subject of a series for his own paper, the *Washington Evening Star*, which acted as a sort of teaser for the longer study and promised to reveal "hidden communities of backwards, illiterate people living in medieval squalor." Even as late as 1935, the *Washington Post* was still reporting the same stories about mountain people who "live in what is probably the most primitive existence in the United States." That story, as Sue Eisenfeld explains in *Shenandoah: A Story of Conversation and Betrayal*, was likely read locally because the *Washington Post* was carried in mountain stores and at the post office.

We can also criticize *Hollow Folk*'s researchers for ignoring another obvious connection—their study began the year the Great Depression arrived and as such, it documents rural families who are navigating the worst years of the nation's worst economic crisis. Casual readers of *Hollow Folk* might have assumed that stock market fluctuations had little impact on the residents of primitive mountain settlements, but that assumption was wrong. Additionally, the Depression had arrived early in the mountains in the form of tree blight and crop failure, from which mountaineers weren't able to recover. Their recovery was impeded not only by the national economic crisis, but also by the fact that the remaining mountain families had a new landlord: the federal government.

After 1933, most of the families remaining in the park were still there because they were too poor to move without assistance. This number included a few hundred tenant families who had not been entitled to compensation for their loss of land and homes. The federal government issued these families special permits that allowed them to remain in the park temporarily but put strict rules in place for their conduct. And like any typical landlord, the government could not resist trying to engage in constructive eviction to speed the process along.

The terms of these new arrangements meant mountaineers could not alter the land in any way without permission. That included chopping wood for fuel, harvesting crops, and even performing regular outdoor work like removing brush. They could not collect apples, which were plentiful in the park and provided mountain families with an important source of income and nutrition. Those who remained in the homes they once owned were not allowed to conduct repairs either, because the condemnation process included properties as well as land. This rule severely disadvantaged mountain families who wanted to move parts of their homesteads outside of the park and rebuild. (My family in Tennessee, for example, survived their own displacement during this time because they were able to deconstruct their home and rebuild it outside the zone of condemnation.) J. Ralph Lassiter, who had been appointed to be the first superintendent of the new park, answered one mountain family's request to collect firewood in the park by stating, "I do not feel that it is our responsibility to furnish them with wood, and I think that the sooner they realize they have to support themselves, the better for all concerned."

Employment also kept people stuck there. Senator Harry Byrd, for example, owned an apple orchard in the mountains and encouraged his workers to remain in place as long as possible to continue serving his operation. For Byrd's workers, this arrangement likely seemed as good as any other, because the future was unpredictable.

During this time, the federal government's plans for displaced families changed dramatically, and after 1933, the large bureaucracy created through Roosevelt's New Deal programs became involved in the eviction process. Thanks to these new programs, and a surplus of labor to run them, the federal government reconsidered its decision to remain uninvolved in the resettlement of mountain families. Time, as always, was of the essence. One welcome development was the creation of a Subsistence Homestead Division that became part of the Department of the Interior, which initiated a Shenandoah Homesteads project in 1934. Under this program, some displaced mountain residents had the opportunity to apply for resettlement on small farms in planned agricultural communities in the five surrounding counties.

But these programs were also created and staffed by individuals who had firm ideas of who they imagined the deserving, and undeserving, poor to be. Young families with children (but not too many children) might go to the front of the line; white families always fared better than Black families. Welfare workers who conducted assessments for eligibility could be impressionable and often used local gossip as part of their decision-making process to eliminate "problem" families. Federal assistance was also means tested. Homesteaders essentially entered into a loan agreement with the federal government and were expected to eventually pay for their new homes. Applicants without some financial means, or a way to prove they could secure work, were ineligible.

For all types of assistance, the federal government demanded cooperation and compliance with the process, which required potential recipients to understand, or pretend to understand, a new and confusing bureaucracy that government workers often did not understand themselves. Mountain residents without allies in the government, and those who couldn't "read" the personalities of decision makers and respond in pleasing or submissive ways, faced an uphill battle.

Mountain families that didn't qualify for assistance from federal programs became the responsibility of the Virginia State Department of Public Welfare, which had the ability to recommend modest state emergency relief aid for families and could conduct its own set of assessments to determine need. Welfare workers also had the option of recommending children be removed into the state's care. They could also escalate concerns about what they considered to be the immoral or illegal activities of adults, which could lead to institutionalization or incarceration.

Elsewhere in Virginia, further south near Blacksburg and beyond the park boundaries, some local residents had come to fear a mercenary tactic employed by state welfare workers informally called "a mountain sweep." It worked like this: with the sheriff's assistance, welfare workers would arrive suddenly in a rural community and, with the element of surprise, order groups of adults and children into waiting vehicles, which would transport them to a local judge for commitment orders or, if the orders had been obtained in advance, directly to an institution. Historian Daniel Kelves, in *In the Name of Eugenics*, quotes a description of these sweeps provided by a former store owner in Montgomery County, Virginia: "Everybody who was drawing welfare then was scared they were going to have it done on them. . . . The sheriff went up there [to Brush Mountain] and loaded all of them in a couple of cars and ran them down to Staunton [Western State Hospital] so they could sterilize them."

To my knowledge, raids like these were not conducted on families living within the park boundaries. But there is evidence that it was a foregone conclusion among state public health and welfare workers that the eviction process would result in the institutionalization of some mountaineers. A local doctor, Roy Sexton, had written to the Park Service promising, "after the survey is done, we'll Colonize the worst of the bunch."

Writing about Minnesota, but with observations equally true of Virginia, historian Molly Ladd-Taylor, in *Fixing the Poor: Eugenic Sterilization and Child Welfare in the Twentieth Century*, argues that eugenics and welfare overlap when "the object of eliminating the so-called unfit converged with keeping taxes and relief costs low, yet at times the welfare goal of providing assistance to the poor and the eugenics goal of reducing their numbers collided." These were heavy tensions that often fell on the shoulders of young, white women new to their careers. Their eagerness to claim a professional identity intersected with a desire to demonstrate common ground with the experts in their field. This common ground was often found in the idea that social problems had biological origins.

———————

After *Hollow Folk*'s publication, Miriam Sizer received additional funding from the state to remain in the Blue Ridge area and assist in the resettlement process. I imagine that she was a jack-of-all-trades by that point, someone who could conduct assessments for relief aid but could also, like her original patron Pollock, act as an intermediary and tour guide of sorts for the various state and federal bureaucrats that arrived in the mountains to manage the poor.

Among mountain families, Sizer suffered guilt by association for her role in *Hollow Folk*'s publication. Locals were aware of the book, and many residents both inside and outside the park resented it. Some of them, tipped off to its conclusions in newspaper articles written by or about the research team, had protested the study so forcefully that Sherman and Henry took the unusual step of answering what they described as a "flood of angry letters" in the book's final text. According to these locals, researchers had proceeded with flawed methods. Their intelligence tests had been devised to study city children, not rural ones. The locals weren't exactly sure what the tests entailed, but they were certain no one would be asking the rural children to identify birds and plants or would be observing the ways they knew the land—qualities, the letter writers argued, that could more accurately measure the children's true aptitude.

Sherman and Henry insisted the researchers had done just that, and the rural children had performed so poorly they not only failed at identifying flora and fauna, but also times of day like morning, noon, and night. "Their way of living does not take into account time or days," Sherman and Henry wrote, explaining that all days must be practically alike when one does nothing of value.

I came to know the Shenandoah Valley families not through *Hollow Folk* but through a collection of photographs produced by a young government photographer named Arthur Rothstein in 1935. Rothstein, working for the Farm Security Administration, had been sent to document the eviction process and create a photographic record of the community before it vanished. When my own family was facing a similar process in Tennessee at this time, waiting to be displaced by the Tennessee Valley Authority, the government sent Lewis Hine to photograph their rural community in its final days. These images were both terrible and wonderful to people in their community. While they captured a moment of enormous loss, they were also the only photographs ever taken of many loved ones. And so I sought out other pictures of soon-to-be-evicted rural families that had been taken by the government photographers, initially motivated by a somewhat selfish and embarrassing desire to claim our photographs, taken by the famous Hine, as the "best" of a grim genre. This is how I first met the Shenandoah families—as the subjects of photographs featuring people who looked and lived like my grandparents in their own uncertain moments of looming finality.

There are two things I might say about the collection of photographs Rothstein produced, and either of them might be true: that he intentionally took unflattering portraits, or that he was simply green and learned best from experimentation. He had a habit of photographing subjects who look posed while the sun is in their eyes and they are squinting or grimacing. At other times, he struggles with angles, shooting children much too high and adults much too low. This makes the camera feel obtrusive, causing subjects to look up or down unnaturally. Whatever the truth is, Rothstein's photographs have always felt off to me, particularly one image he took of what appears to be a mother and daughter.

We first see the mother, identified as Fannie Corbin in the photo's title, in the center of the frame. Her hair is pinned high and she is smooth-aproned. The sleeves of her blouse are pushed up to her elbows, and her hands grip the short banisters on either side of the five steps that lead up to her covered porch, where some of her younger children sit in the shade. A teenage daughter, who I later learned was called Mollie, stands behind her, equally neat in a belted dress and hat. Mollie's pose is more relaxed than her mother's, but if you look closely at her feet, you can see that the heel of her left foot is resting on the step above where she is standing. Fannie is staring directly into the camera, her left arm cutting across Mollie's body. This is an image of discomfort and retreat.

Years later, I would learn, from Richard Knox Robinson's *Rothstein's First Assignment*, a documentary produced about the images, that Rothstein often traveled with Sizer as he toured the settlements. Rothstein suggests that Sizer's presence, and her pride in her contributions to *Hollow Folk*, perhaps led to some of the narratives his images convey, most obviously in the short descriptions that made their way into the captions of Rothstein's photographs. One child is captioned as a "halfwit;" another a "girl who is about sixteen but has the mentality of a child of seven." One adult woman is described by her (preposterous) fertility—the "mother of 22 children"—while an elderly woman is identified as "Mrs. Eddie Nicholson, who frequently goes to the resort to beg."

Katrina Powell also found Sizer in a silent film produced by the government in 1936 titled *A Trip to Shenandoah.* Powell writes, "Sizer is seen holding onto the neck of a child, presumably to keep him still for the camera, while talking about and pointing to the child's body. . . . Though there is no verbal narrative in the film, one conclusion that can be drawn is that the removal of the child and care under the state will result in better health."

We do not know if Sizer was also present when Rothstein made his images of Fannie and Mollie Corbin in 1935. Sue Currell, who writes about the connections between eugenics and documentary photography, has a different explanation for the uncomfortable image, which is based on a devastating piece of information I did not know until she published her essay, "You Haven't Seen Their Faces," in 2017.

Currell's work reveals that by the time Rothstein photographed the Corbin women, social workers had arranged for Mollie to be sterilized at the Lynchburg Colony. "The photograph of Fannie Corbin with her daughter Mollie," she writes, "thus captures the young woman in the period between her clinical assessment as an 'imbecile' and her incarceration for sterilization, which a State Hospital Board discharge certificate shows to have lasted until June 1940." These findings add chilling detail to the information, including a mysterious letter from local doctor Roy Sexton that Robinson discovered during the making of his documentary: as many as eleven members of the Corbin family were committed between 1935 and 1942, nine of them children.

And so "Fannie's weary look," Currell suggests, "reflects

the fact that, for over five years, they had been visited, inspected, watched, photographed, and evicted—and none of it had provided them with the new homes and new lives that they had been promised and so desperately needed."

———————————

I do not know what happened to Mollie Corbin after 1940. But I know what happened to her younger cousin Mary Frances, who was possibly one of the last children born into what is now Shenandoah National Park. I know what happened to her because Mary eventually became an advocate for people who, like her and like Mollie, had been committed and sterilized as children.

Mary did not recall much about living in what is now the national park. This is what she remembered instead. She remembered that her family did not survive long after relocation and that she was taken away to the Lynchburg Colony. There, when she was eleven years old, she had an operation where something went badly wrong. She remembered a nurse telling her it was all in God's hands. Still, she recovered and understood she had been sterilized. That's not something every patient could say, not because they were feebleminded, but because staff often hid it from them by pretending patients had simply undergone surgery to remove an appendix.

Mary remembered that for the majority of her almost sixteen years at the Colony, she was forced to clean and bathe other patients. If she didn't do a good job, staff made her sleep with an incontinent resident or locked her in a small room with someone prone to violence. She remembered her first taste of paid work, earning $1 a month to clean potatoes in the institution's kitchen. It was a trial run for life outside of the facility, which was coming because Mary had now "improved" from the feeblemindedness the state once argued was a permanent condition. In truth, it did not matter to the state if Mary had improved or not. She had survived into the era of deinstitutionalization, when states began releasing long-stay psychiatric patients to save money. Adult patients like Mary, infertile and compliant, made ideal candidates to return to society.

Mary eventually broke her silence for *The Lynchburg Story*. She also appeared in Mary Carter Bishop's investigation, "An Elite Said Their Kind Wasn't Wanted," in the *Roanoke Times*. She described to Bishop how terrifying those first years of freedom were even though she found jobs and enjoyed independence. When she didn't work hard enough, her employers threatened to send her back to the Colony. She lived with the fear that it could all be taken away again.

Mary certainly remembered what she called the best time of her life: being married. In 1958, a few years after her release from the Lynchburg Colony, she married Robert Donald. It was a gift to Mary to find a husband who accepted the fact that she could not have children, and she believed she found that in Robert. They had ten good years of marriage. And then Robert left her. Mary always believed he changed his mind about children. "That's the end of that story now," she said.

Mary died on April 14, 2015. I do not know who wrote her obituary in the *Madison County Eagle*, but there is a righteousness to it. The writer calls *Hollow Folk* a "discredited ethnographic study," then goes on to explain:

> From the forced eviction from her mountain home, where Hollow Folk "found" that the "problems" of the Corbins were due to their isolation from society—providing justification for the condemnation of their land to make way for the Shenandoah National Park. To the forced institutionalization and sterilization of many of

her family members—where it was "determined" that many of the Corbin children were "unfit" to have children. Hollow Folk and the government programs that used it had a devastating impact on her family.

It is extremely rare to see scare quotes or the phrase "discredited ethnographic study" in an obituary. But why not assign blame? We are too hung up on forgiveness, on letting the past lie. I prefer Mary's version of events; the flat truth. It is better than the way that some Charlottesville leaders tried to memorialize Carrie Buck as a woman who had earned back her productivity as a hard worker and good citizen.

As the obituary continues, here is how Mary wanted us to remember her: "Mary played an important role in bringing Virginia's eugenics program to an end. . . . Mary and a handful of her friends from 'The Colony' found the strength to confront this legacy. Traveling to Richmond to protest eugenics to the governor, they were able to end the government program that had so impacted their lives." Mary spoke openly of her pain to filmmakers, reporters, researchers, and disability rights advocates. She left a generous record behind so that others would know what children like her experienced at the Colony.

These were the kind of people that Joseph DeJarnette claimed had no right to be born and should be weeded from Virginia. Fitting that Western State should now have a garden full of weeds.

One day, in a kinder world, we might at last claim who is buried beneath them.

CHAPTER FOUR:

THE PATIENT IS GOOD FOR WORK, AND WORK IS GOOD FOR THE PATIENT

It is spring, and the city is a wedding day. Crisp white tents go up on the lawn of Western State Hospital in Staunton, Virginia, a hospital that isn't a hospital anymore, but a fine hotel. The sun warms the bricks and the mountain. The bride comes. Here are new beginnings. All that is painful can be left behind. After all, asylums were places of forgetting, were they not? At least that was the hope. In 1824, Virginia chose Staunton as the site for a new hospital because of the city's proximity to rural nothingness. Housing patients there meant they might be better able to forget their own suffering. It also made it easier for society to forget its "dangerous, ungovernable, and offensive members." In *Madness and Civilization*, philosopher Michel Foucault writes, "The country, by the gentleness and variety of its landscapes, wins melancholics from their single obsession." In the earliest years of Western State, perhaps that was true.

And who knows? Maybe it is fitting to hold a wedding there now. Maybe I'm wrong about this place. After all, the site has all the qualities of a church, doesn't it? Think of all the souls that received transformation there. Think of the nearby graves and the little chapel that once stood on the premises. That building too will be repurposed, surely; a notable architect designed it. Someone will find profit in those old bones. Until then, though, we can gather its lessons and give them out freely: *Whatever God has joined together, let no man put asunder.*

In the spring of 1931, Patient 18235 at Western State Hospital received that same lesson one morning, although she never knew it. Eighty-seven years later in the Library of Virginia's sunny reading room, I read the official record of her sterilization. In the margins, I traced with my finger an odd line that had been written by an unknown hand: *Whatever God has joined together, let no man put asunder.* Then, underneath it: *May God forgive.* What do these lines mean? Were they written with tenderness or contempt for the patient? What had been joined together? Who committed the trespass that needed forgiveness? If, on that morning, Joseph DeJarnette, the superintendent, had decided to improve a building instead of a woman, then I might better know the full history of that day.

Once, without catching it, I misspoke when I told someone else about these lines. I told them the archival record said, "May God forgive us." In one small slip of the tongue, I invented an alternate history for Western State, one where physicians felt hesitant or contrite about the harm they inflicted on their patients. I rewrote the place through a single pronoun.

But no matter. The kind of history that surrounds a place like Western State Hospital is always at the mercy of revision.

In 2003, the city of Staunton began confronting a thorny question: What is a small and historically minded community supposed to do with a place like Western State Hospital?

Western State opened in 1828 as the Western State Lunatic Asylum. Gluttonous for land to accommodate its expanding patient population, its growth peaked after World War II when it encompassed 1,300 acres in the heart of the city. Over time, it became more like a kingdom than a hospital. Its landholdings included well-producing farmland, pleasure gardens, watersheds, workhouses, treatment facilities, dormitories, and homes for staff. Today, the fringes of the former hospital rest gently at the more urban end of Staunton, nestled at the foot of the city's modern downtown core.

The hospital arrived during an era of institution building in Virginia. In Staunton, that also materialized as Mary Baldwin University, a former women's college founded in 1842, and the Virginia School for the Deaf and Blind, which was established in 1839. The city's development is intractably linked to these three institutions, which all, in their own way, were created to serve people on the margins of society. It's a unique identity and purpose that sometimes situates Staunton within a progressive history. But at other times, it marks it as a place where people undoubtedly ignored, or participated in, abusive practices toward vulnerable populations.

Western State's original campus ceased to be a hospital in the 1970s after its operations transitioned slowly to a new facility three miles away. In 1981, the Virginia Department of Corrections took over the original site, and the state turned parts of it into the Staunton Correctional Center, a medium-security men's prison. This repurposing didn't require many updates, but the state conducted enough structural stabilization work on key buildings to keep them functional until 2003. At that point, the prison closed, and the title transferred to the city, which netted about eighty acres of land filled with an assembly of buildings reflecting a range of dates and purposes.

The wider county is still home to a number of correctional facilities and enterprises. And though I tend to use the word "controversial" generously when I'm describing any correctional facility, here that descriptor seems especially accurate. In 2018, for example, the local Shenandoah Valley Juvenile Justice Center underwent state review amid allegations that workers had employed "restraint techniques," including blindfolding and beating children. At the Augusta Correctional Center, located about a half hour away in Craigsville, long-standing staff shortages and deplorable conditions frequently make the local news. Libre by Nexus, a local enterprise that opened in 2014, is currently embroiled in a number of lawsuits connected to its profit-driven model of offering bail services for immigrants. In November 2018, the modern-day Western State Hospital settled a $900,000 lawsuit with the family of an elderly psychiatric patient who claimed the hospital had denied her basic human dignity to such an extent that it resulted in her untimely death. All of these ventures tend to attribute their failings to the pressures of operating on a shoestring budget following reduction after reduction in state funding.

Scandals like these lurk in the background of any community with similar facilities. But in Staunton they impinge upon the city's reputation and preferred identity as a quaint tourist destination. The city, I think, wants to be a place where national park visitors day-trip for antiquing and tasty lunches, not a community with a long, reverberating history of confining people. This is understandable, but that impulse also puts Staunton at odds with its own past. And that past, or at least the more anodyne version of it consumed by visitors who come to be impressed by the city's well-preserved architecture and historic landscape, is what fuels its tourism industry and much of its economic growth today.

That the original Western State Hospital, located so closely to the crown jewel of the city's downtown, should eventually become part of Staunton's growing tourist economy was almost a foregone conclusion. But the challenge was finding a partner who had enough capital and creativity to execute an appropriate vision for the site's new chapter. After vetting a number of potential candidates, the city transferred Western

State's title in 2006 to Richmond-based developers Robin Miller and Dan Gecker. The two men anticipated the project would cost $250 million, and the success of their pitch rested on two well-defined, initial phases for redevelopment—transforming key structures on the campus into high-end condominiums, the Villages at Staunton, and then, reinvesting the profits from those sales to create a luxury hotel, the Blackburn Inn. The plans also called for an additional three phases—including the construction of new homes, office spaces, and retail sites on the land that was included in the transfer—but those were less defined. Over the last fourteen years, phases one and two have come to fruition as exactly as they were initially described; the condominiums began to go on the market around 2008, and the hotel arrived in 2018.

My own arrival in Staunton occurred in 2016 when my partner Josh and I decided to do the move-back-home-but-up-the-road-a-bit thing. I guess you could say we were in need of some healing landscapes. But my first inkling that things in the city had changed happened a little earlier and at a distance, when we were looking for a place to live and I began navigating real estate websites to get reacquainted with the area. Writing this four years later, it's strange to think that my first reaction to Western State's renovation was a fit of dismissive laughter, when a website asked me if I was interested in paying $500,000 to live in that shithole.

Here is the part of this book that will probably get me excommunicated from Staunton, where I describe the redeveloped Western State as, above all else, an architecturally sublime honey trap for boomers. But please, I am only borrowing directly from Robin Miller's own vision, which explicitly stated that the market for his real estate offerings was focused on "people who live outside the area who are looking for a place to retire or a second home." Miller was quite right that marketing the site to local residents would not be sustainable. New properties at the Villages at Staunton are priced between $250,000 and $500,000, while Staunton's median household income hovers around $45,000 per year. I watched the project develop from my vantage point in the city, a historic home Josh and I rented from a landlord who rode around town in a pick-up truck with an "I Brake for Old Houses" bumper sticker and who didn't care that the ones she rented out had holes in the floor.

———————

In 2012, journalist Logan Ward, writing for the National Trust for Historic Preservation, suggested that "all you have to do is look around at the beautifully maintained buildings designed in an eclectic mix of architectural styles to realize that historic preservation drove Staunton's renaissance." Since 2000, as he notes, "more than $50 million in private investment—from single-family homes to mixed-use commercial projects—has poured into the city." Bill Hamilton, Staunton's economic development director, happily agreed. "Historic preservation is such an important part of who we are in Staunton," he said, "that you can't separate it from the city's economic growth."

The story of how that reality came to be goes like this. In the 1980s, a fever for small town historic preservation began sweeping the country. Led by the National Trust for Historic Preservation, the idea emerged that, following a decade of recession, communities might be able to revitalize their local economies by using preservation-focused development. The classic example would involve something like a pokey downtown hardware store—long abandoned from its original purpose and a bit blighted—returning to use as another income-producing business, like a restaurant or (because it was the eighties) a tanning salon. Of course, business owners who were willing to take on less than perfect properties required some incentives. Those came in the form of federal and state tax credits, which the Trust coached communities on how to navigate and utilize.

Staunton caught the fever for preservation early on. Thanks to a few committed architectural history enthusiasts, the city became what is known as a Main Street Community in 1985, a designation that signals it is working closely with the National Trust. Today, our "Main Street" (which is actually named Beverley) has theaters, restaurants, art galleries, boutiques, and professional services, all veneered with a mostly coherent architectural vision that emphasizes the buildings' Victorian pedigree. This has made Staunton into a city of lovely façades. The tourist literature refers to it as an "ideal base," a place to relax in between hardier adventures, perhaps in the nearby Shenandoah National Park. That reputation anchors a steadily rising tourism economy that is currently worth around $56 million a year.

At its best, historic preservation has a deeply civic purpose that is less connected to landmarking old buildings and more attuned to the gentle work of encouraging communities to be thoughtful about what they want to be. We are only temporary custodians of the places we live, the thinking goes, and historic preservation inserts callouts to that reality within communities, tempering impulses from generation to generation to constantly remake and transform a place.

But historic preservation has another side too. It can sometimes function as a kind of disaster capitalism, where a loss in the past becomes a gain for developers in the present. Tax credit schemes and the initial funding required to rehabilitate challenging properties can embed preservation within a complex economic system most easily navigated by consultants, investors, lawyers, and architects. This means that some types of historic preservation will always fall more squarely within the world of high-stakes property development. On the one hand, this is an ordinary tension within many communities—How much of a city should a single developer be allowed to own?—but on the other, it attempts to resolve that tension by borrowing the reputation of historic preservation as a civic good.

When I trained in historic preservation, one of our key texts was a modest technical guide called *The Economics of Historic Preservation*. Written by Donovan Rypkema, a real estate appraiser turned preservationist, the book transformed the field after its publication in 1994. Rypkema's guide is coaching material; it includes data intended to help preservationists talk convincingly about things like rates of return, property values, and tax credits. But its biggest contribution was the way it took the National Trust's philosophy and injected it with steroids, positioning historic preservation as a solution to a wide array of economic challenges faced by communities. Do you want job creation? Historic preservation yields attractive spaces for new businesses and keeps tradespeople and vendors employed. Is there a lack of affordable housing in your community? It's easier and cheaper to rehabilitate older, unoccupied homes than to build new ones. Are energy costs soaring? Historic properties are more energy efficient. Rypkema, and those who followed in his footsteps, helped transform the very nature of historic preservation, turning it into a type of architectural cure-all whose vision was focused on the future, not just the past.

Two decades later, one legacy of Rypkema's work is that historic preservationists can now talk comfortably about economics, property development, assets, markets, revenue, and revitalization. But they rarely talk about capitalism. If anything, there's a tendency to see historic preservation as a reaction *against* capitalism, a civic act that protects people and places from economic exploitation by emphasizing sustainability over quick profit.

When I first visited Staunton, as just someone passing

through for a lazy lunch while making the rounds among family, I believed the city had discovered the magic of staying true to historical preservation at its best, which is no easy task.

But then I moved here and became neighbors with Western State.

———

This might be the part of book where you feel like saying, "This is all good, but where is the actual history of Western State? You've only told us about one superintendent, and here, in this chapter about the hospital, it seems like the right place to at least give something of a bare bones account of the rest of the site's past, doesn't it?"

That is the exact question I have asked myself every day for four years: Where is Western State's history?

And I don't mean to be pedantic here, but I need to explain that trying to answer one question—*Where is Western State's history?*—is not the same as answering another one— *What is Western State's history?* The *where* always leads to the *what*, but there is a powerful degree of difference between the two. Where, for example, is the history of enslavement in the United States? According to many people who currently own and operate historic plantations, it is not to be found at their sites. Often, these owners and operators justify their interpretive choices by arguing that the history of enslavement can be found in other places, including academic scholarship. But in cases like these, denying the *where* is an intentional strategy to prevent us from getting to the *what*, which would mean identifying these historical properties not just as architectural monuments, but as sites of trauma.

In the public historian's lingo, we often call this strategy "silencing the past." We do so in honor of a foundational text by the same name, Michel-Rolph Trouillot's 1995 study *Silencing the Past: Power and the Production of History.* Trouillot's book discusses a phenomenon long observed and commented on, but rarely explained with such clarity; that the information recorded or omitted in a historical narrative reflects a struggle for power. Trouillot, a Haitian anthropologist, argues that by making this struggle visible, *by admitting it exists*, we can unlock deeper understandings not only of the past, but also about how power works in our contemporary world.

"We are never as steeped in history as when we pretend not to be," Trouillot writes. And so, when I began to ask myself where the history of Western State is, I also have to ask myself where it isn't, and why.

As a prerequisite to writing this book, my publisher Anne convinced me to spend a night at the Blackburn Inn about six months after it opened. The excursion was intended to supplement the occasions I'd visited the site previously— as a diner at the hotel's restaurant—and to interrupt my unproductive habit of simply glaring at it during my commute. It helped that Anne agreed to keep me company, along with my partner.

When we arrived for our stay, I didn't wander about the hotel and grounds with old architectural plans and historical documents, morbidly pointing out "*That's where they cut people up!*" to anyone who had the misfortune of speaking to me. I didn't even do this to Anne, who might have tolerated a sinister aside like this as proof I was working. I also didn't unleash delicious indignation when we arrived and weren't immediately greeted by some poorly assembled exhibit detailing Western State's darker history or when we found out the hotel wasn't offering a "Worst Moments in Psychiatric Medicine" tour.

Because of my work as a public historian, I've visited many places that feel like the new Western State feels—it's helped me develop low expectations and a strong constitution. I've spent the night at former prisons, plantations, and asylums. I've handled equipment used to hurt people and even put them to death. I am not trying to make myself sound tough. I'm only stressing that I can compartmentalize the gruesome history of places when needs must, and I am usually good at it.

But spending a night at the Blackburn Inn made me nervous. I wasn't afraid of dark histories and ghosts, but I was dreading the moment when I'd have to admit that, from the perspective of the architectural sublime, the developers had really nailed it. And look, I'll admit the hotel is really nice. It's really fucking nice. And it's also kind of cozy? After my stay, I even went home and purchased a blanket identical to the ones used on the hotel's beds.

———

That former asylums should be examples of both architectural masterwork and sites of trauma is a duality that many preservationists feel we are overdue to reconcile. Their calls for the adaptation of sites like Western State often use the example of what are called Kirkbride Buildings, named for physician and architect Thomas Story Kirkbride. Starting around 1840, Kirkbride had created an asylum design plan that harmonized the built environment of hospitals with the growing movement of physicians and reformers who wanted to move psychiatric medicine in a more humane direction. Kirkbride's architectural plans emphasized ways to increase comforts and provide fresh air, sunlight, and adequate hygiene. In all, his ideas were used to build around seventy hospitals in the United States, which have proved, in their afterlife as disused buildings, to be difficult to deal with by the communities where they are located. About a dozen of them currently remain standing throughout the United States.

Kirkbride Buildings have hardcore fans, including

preservationists, photographers, and even ghost hunters. These people all make the same case when they argue we should save what's left of the buildings. When we lose these sites, they claim, we are losing a vital link to a collective past. Some even suggest that myths about early mental health treatment endanger these buildings just as much as neglect. The stigma about treatments that now seem barbaric, the thinking goes, obscures the fact that these facilities were actually designed to help people. As photographer and preservation advocate Ian Ference argued in a 2017 TEDx talk, "Sure there were cold water baths, there were forcible shower rooms where patients were lashed up and a hose was turned on them, and there were various shock therapies—most notably electro-convulsive therapy—but the main story is about the optimism of the asylum during the asylum period."

Where these enthusiasts can disagree, or at least run out of answers, is what to do with these buildings if the calls to save them are successful. To be fair, it's not an easy question to answer at all. Most favor projects that do some justice to the history of the building's original use. Robert Kirkbride, an architect who is in fact related to Thomas and who is active in the preservation of his buildings, points to the success of Oregon State Hospital's redevelopment. Part of its original campus became the Oregon State Museum of Mental Health, which features a memorial space for former patients, including a room that contains the unclaimed ashes of 3,500 people who died at the site. But converting these buildings into museums isn't an attractive option for developers who are spending millions of dollars on renovations. And to be honest, sometimes commercial development is the only strategy that makes financial sense. Still, Robert Kirkbride encourages planners and developers to find ways to explain and build context for the site's history and, ideally, to be open to the idea that, in finding a new purpose, they shouldn't erase the building's past.

Western State is not a Kirkbride building, although it grew out of a similar design philosophy. According to the developers, though, it is actually something better because it has a connection to Thomas Jefferson, which in Virginia is worth its weight in gold. And it is through this Jefferson connection that we at last get to find Western State's history, or part of it, in the story developers tell to explain the site's architectural pedigree.

At the hotel, as Anne happily slept in her room in a bed so comfortable we still marvel at it today, I was in my room cobbling together the developers' master narrative of the site from the property's branding material and the websites for the Blackburn Inn and the Villages at Staunton. I reread interviews the developers had given with local papers to get a sense of what features or stories about the site were most important to them.

In their version of events, the story of Western State Hospital really begins in 1840, when a brilliant, young physician named Dr. Francis T. Stribling became the superintendent of what was then the Western State Lunatic Asylum. Stribling was a local boy fresh from the University of Pennsylvania Medical School. Once he came back to Staunton, he inherited from his predecessor a hospital that was not even ten years old and was still very much an architectural work in progress. Influenced by Kirkbride (who had also attended the University of Pennsylvania) and his own philosophies of patient care, Stribling became convinced that architecture could be an important ally in the treatment of mental illness.

Stribling became the superintendent at Western State during a turning point in the field of psychiatric medicine. Up to this point, patients were often treated like criminals, restrained for the ease of staff, and placed in an environment that had the features of a prison. Optimism about potential cures was rare; instead, patients were treated like difficult animals, receiving only the barest attention to their needs and comforts. Stribling and his colleagues were convinced a break from the past was necessary, however, and in his first year as superintendent, he vowed to meet patients "as friends and brothers" and to "inquire whether, by a system of moral means, not less extensive than human, we may not be enabled to eradicate their disease and restore them again to all the privileges and enjoyments of rational beings."

Stribling believed there could be no worse place for a patient than a jail or almshouse, and he took great pains to ensure Western State did not resemble institutions of that type. This philosophy, and its execution, became typical of what is remembered as the era of moral medicine, in which humane treatment supplanted absolute confinement and physical restraint. "We treat them," Stribling wrote in 1837, referring to patients, "as human beings deserving of attention and care, rather than criminals and outlaws, meriting not even our compassion." Because he wanted his patients to return to society, he hoped to accelerate their healing, or at the very least not worsen their distress, by designing a pleasant hospital core and emphasizing access to natural beauty. Of course, Stribling's theories about moral medicine only extended to white patients and enslaved workers, first those he personally leased to the site and then later purchased for the hospital, ensured Western State remained pleasant through their domestic labor. An acknowledgment of their presence and labors is absent from recirculated tales about this earlier era.

When Stribling turned to the task of expanding Western State, an architect named Thomas Blackburn helped him translate these desires into brick and mortar. Blackburn had previously worked under Thomas Jefferson during the construction of the University of Virginia. He applied the skills he gained during that experience to create magnificent designs that were attentive to Stribling's requests that patients have access to ample fresh air and light, opportunities to look at a variety of landscapes, and a selection of comforts like stately pleasure grounds. Together, the two men worked to produce Western State's most interesting and oldest structures, including what is now the Blackburn Inn. Their partnership was fruitful and long, lasting until 1858 or 1859, and Stribling remained as Western State's superintendent until his death in 1874.

On the website for the Blackburn Inn today, under the section labeled, "History of the Inn," there are about 300 words dedicated to the site's past. The majority of them are about Stribling's important role in the hospital's development (though the site does misspell his name at one point), describing him as a man who believed in "what he called 'moral treatment' which focused on the emotional well-being of patients." The hotel's account also highlights the various architectural details from Stribling's tenure that guests might observe today. "Together, Stribling and Blackburn also added spacious room wings, magnificent gardens, and a hand-crafted spiral staircase leading to a cupola and rooftop veranda."

The next section of the inn's narrative then conspicuously skips forward in time:

> Western State Hospital later relocated, and the original property was transformed into a medium-security prison in 1981. Edward Murray, the first superintendent of the correctional facility, appreciated the beautiful landscape and although some prison infrastructure had to be constructed on site, Murray preserved as much of the original property as he could.

> Once the correctional facility closed, the city of Staunton took over ownership and began searching for a developer to restore the historic buildings and grounds. Richmond-based firm, Miller and Associates, proved to the city that they could take on the task. In 2006, Miller and Associates, became the new owners of the 80-acre property or what is now known as The Villages of Staunton [*sic*], an upscale, mixed-use community.

You might notice there is a one-hundred-year gap between the Stribling era and 1981. That gap also appears in the branding information for the Villages at Staunton. The websites of both enterprises link back and forth. Guests like me who are cozy in bed—thinking, *Why not make this a permanent thing?*—can just pull up the hotel website and click right over to properties, the marketing logic probably goes. Will I know that the gap in the history the websites present includes Western State's post-Civil War reorganization, its eugenics era, and the eventual move to deinstitutionalization? I think the better question is: Would I even care?

There are two specific stories about the Stribling era that do an excellent job of collapsing past and present, which is perhaps why they are circulated now; to smooth that gap. The first comes from community chatter I heard when I first moved to Staunton. The story goes that families from out of town who were shepherding their daughters to Mary Baldwin University sometimes took them to Western State by mistake. If the story's true, some of the confusion could be explained by the fact that the college and the hospital are close to one another. But the real gist of the story is that these parents were totally content, until someone corrected them, to leave young women at the site because it was indistinguishable from a picturesque and newly built university. It was not, in other words, a gloomy place with distressed, hovering patients, but instead a setting that invited parents to imagine their children happily thriving there.

The developers tell a similar story that emphasizes how happy things once were. Drawing attention to some of the site's minor architectural details, Dan Gecker suggested to a reporter from the *Richmond Times-Dispatch* that, "The site was so beautiful that a fence surrounding the property was not meant to keep residents in, but to keep townspeople from going on picnics on the campus, or so the legend goes." This legend happens to be true. In 1848, staff took out notice in the local paper forbidding the public from recreation-seeking on the hospital grounds, which included a lush, park-like lawn. Around 1855, an ornamental iron fence—not exactly unassailable, but with short, pointy spikes designed to convey "Keep Out"—went up. It still stands today.

Both of these stories are about so-called normal people in Staunton, both visitors and residents, who wanted access to Western State because of its sublime landscape and beautiful buildings. Because the redeveloped site is marketed on the basis of those now restored sublime landscapes and beautiful buildings, it's a sly way to connect Western State's old and new identities. But the best part, of course, is left implied by the developers—that thanks to their efforts, we no longer have to be jealous townspeople excluded from this wonderful place by the accident of our sound minds. Now, for the right price, we're more than welcome inside those iron gates.

"But why present the fence story as a legend?" I wondered, now half-asleep in my room at the Blackburn Inn and feeling the pull of oblivion from my comfortable bed. In order to claim tax credits, the developers had been required to submit an inventory and descriptions of such details to the government, so it's hard to imagine Miller and Gecker didn't know the fence's actual pedigree. Does framing it as a legend just make for better branding? Maybe. But could it also be a subtle way of suggesting *there is so much history here and how can we ever possibly know it all?*

––––––––––––

To begin filling in the hundred-year gap in the developers' history, we could start with a structure known as the Wheary Building. In 2008, developers confirmed Western State's rebirth by affixing a marquee here, visible from the city's main artery, that advertised CONDOS FOR SALE. Just two short years after the complex changed hands, the first renovated properties in the Villages at Staunton were on the market. These included units in the Wheary, which was being rechristened as the Lofts.

The speed of the transformation is a testament to the skill of the developers' team. But the developers' decision to launch their real estate venture with the restoration of a collection of structures that included the Wheary was also a practical choice related to the buildings' condition. The Department of Corrections had utilized these buildings between 1981 and 2003, which meant that some of the utilities had been modernized and the buildings in general were less neglected. Starting the restoration there would be considerably easier, it would produce assets for market turnaround, and the profits could begin recirculating through the bloodstream of the rest of the project.

But contrary to what the hotel's website might suggest, this decision also meant that the restored Western State's first flowers did not bloom from a building designed by Francis Stribling and Thomas Blackburn. The Wheary Building had been constructed in 1935, and it had been designed by Joseph DeJarnette.

DeJarnette, whose tenure as Western State's superintendent

bested Stribling's by three years, also had a design philosophy he executed at the hospital. Like his more celebrated predecessor, that philosophy was inspired by his own view of patients. Between 1905 and 1943, DeJarnette used this philosophy to guide his arrangement of Western State's physical world. He altered and created buildings, managed and grew Western State's landholdings, and, perhaps even more than Stribling, used this environment in the service of treatments he claimed were therapeutic. This design philosophy was eugenics.

Eugenics has always aimed to breed better humans. But for its early twentieth-century adherents, it was also, strangely, a language of hope. *If we persist in our goal in the present*, they thought, *one day the world will find order.* We now understand their goal best as a quest for racial and genetic purity, but they knew that goal's ultimate achievement lay beyond their lifetimes. In the meantime, practicing eugenicists like DeJarnette had to build their order out of the broken pieces of people who had no right, in his estimation, to be alive and yet were. And if genetic purity wasn't possible in the short-term, perhaps economic purity could serve as a consolation prize.

DeJarnette believed that his patients had reached the innate limits of their biology and could not progress further through the efforts of science or medicine. He dreamed of their elimination. In 1934, he tallied that 56,244 people had been sterilized in Germany in the first year under the country's new Law for the Prevention of Hereditarily Diseased Offspring. He smarted, "the Germans are beating us at our own game." He had no hope of catching up. But at the end of his career, he boasted to the *News Leader* that the Virginia sterilization law he championed in 1924 had been applied to 4,604 people and that he could claim 1,205 of those procedures. He estimated he had helped prevent the births of 138,130 defective children. Surely, he thought, that was worth something.

When DeJarnette made statements like this about the

worth of his actions, he was often preparing to value them quite literally. In his mind, had those defective children been allowed to live, they would have had a negative value of two million dollars. Through their elimination, however, DeJarnette claimed their negative value as a positive one, rendered in savings to the state and society by the fact of their absence. How did he arrive at his figures? Part of his tabulations included what he estimated to be the cost of their lifetime confinement in state hospitals, which he based on his own figures from Western State. But he also extrapolated wildly based on what he thought their potential to cause damage through crime might be, or how much charitable or public assistance they might claim.

This was just the start. DeJarnette's math was also intended to invite his contemporaries into a world where these debts reproduced with the debtor. He often used popular eugenic texts to justify his figures. His preferred study was Henry Goddard's *The Kallikak Family: A Study in the Heredity of Feeblemindedness* from 1912, which propelled the highly fictionalized family to eugenic fame. Goddard's book tells the story of Martin Kallikak, a virtuous man and Revolutionary War hero. Though Martin is married to a Quaker woman, in a fit of post-battle horniness, he surrenders to the charms of a low-life tavern maid. She becomes pregnant and gives birth to a son who, like its mother, is feebleminded. This is no matter for Martin, however. He goes on with his life, returns to his upstanding marriage, and fills his family tree with the fruit of normal children. It's a happy ending for Martin, but not for society.

As *The Kallikak Family* explains, Martin's illegitimate, feebleminded son goes on to produce feebleminded children of his own. By the time we arrive in the present, that one tryst has produced a total of 480 descendants. According to Goddard, 143 of these were also feebleminded, including a woman he called "Deborah Kallikak," who was confined to the New Jersey Home for the Education and Care of Feebleminded Children, the institution he managed. Goddard provides details about Deborah's life at the institution, working at a sewing machine or as a waitress. He includes long descriptions of her feeblemindedness, which had produced "no noticeable defect" and had not impaired her ability to "run an electric sewing machine, cook, and do practically everything about the house."

Deborah Kallikak, whose real name was Emma Wolverton, had been institutionalized as a ward of the state when she was eight years old. Her aptitudes, Goddard warns, should not be taken as proof that she might function well if she were released from care. She would instead lead a life "that would be vicious, immoral, and criminal, though because of her mentality she herself would not be responsible." This is just the burden of the feebleminded, Goddard explains, which is exacerbated by the fact that "a large portion of those who are considered feebleminded . . . would not be recognized as such by the untrained observer." Poor Martin, for example, had no way of knowing he was bedding a defective. Goddard includes some mild sermonizing toward men of good families to temper their animal urges. But the more practical solution, he argues, is the sterilization of the unfit.

Although Goddard defended his study for the next thirty years, he was also one of the rarer eugenicists who interrogated some facets of his beliefs over time. Paul Lombardo finds, for example, that by 1927, as Goddard's work became foundational to securing the verdict in *Buck v. Bell*, Goddard himself was questioning if there were inaccuracies in contemporary clinical definitions of feeblemindedness. Many soldiers who enlisted during World War I, for example, had scores similar to feebleminded people based on intelligence tests administered by the Army. Perhaps the standards needed to be recalibrated.

Joseph DeJarnette, however, entertained no such flexibility. "Assuming that each sterilized person would have 30 descendants in five generations, and well known John Kallikak had 490 descendants in five generations, it means that we have cut out potentially 60,000 defectives," he estimated in 1935, based on the 2,203 sterilizations performed by the state up to that point. "Assuming each of these defectives would have had 30 descendants and 20 years of life it would equal 1,200,000 supported in Virginia one year during five generations, and estimating the cost of support at $150.00 per year it means a savings to the state of $180,000,000." This is dizzying, typical DeJarnette math.

DeJarnette's idea of economic purity looked like a balance sheet wiped clean of the debts people like Deborah Kallikak and Carrie Buck inflicted on society. He fixated on controlling these numbers, perpetually calibrating the rate of return on his actions. One half of the population will be insane by 2000, he tabulated in one set of notes, but with sterilization, none of us might be. He was meticulous in the figures of his own life, too, recording the number of apples he purchased on a journey and the cost of his daily newspapers. Each day, new numbers. Each day, a chance for balance and order. Each day to the hospital where the numbers lived, each year ever more of them arriving.

Order, however, remained elusive. The pleasure of an ultimate tabulation was always deferred to someone else, a member of a future generation who would arrive in the world and hopefully find the slate wiped clean. Through his frenzied math, DeJarnette convinced himself that all would be well eventually. Yet where could he find his own satisfaction? Where could the order he craved be made real? By helping expand society's definitions of the unfit, by arguing their ever growing and costly threat, he was now awash in debts incurred by their confinement and care. What ledger book could ever balance such a paradox?

Western State could. "In my opinion," DeJarnette wrote in 1921, three years before the passage of Virginia's sterilization law, "the most humane and practical methods for handling the unfit is sterilization." Then, as an afterthought he added: "According to Mendel's Law, a large number of this class are as much manufactured articles as plows and harrows." But plows and harrows are strong tools.

Three years later finds him testifying as an expert witness to advance the state's case that Carrie Buck should be sterilized. Why should the state permit itself to force this young woman into permanent infertility? "It benefits society by not taking care of them, and by the work they do," he answers. "They are the hewers of wood and drawers of water." It is better not to interrupt the domestic work of these women, his colleague Albert Priddy later testified in answer to the same question. "People don't care to take them when there is a constant chance of them becoming mothers."

The state might be able to reach total economic perfection by eliminating the social debt of the unfit through sterilization, but until that happened, eugenic sterilization could also create a more productive underclass of menial workers whose labor could benefit purer Virginians. This logic could also be applied to people who did not need to be sterilized because their lives were led in confinement. They too could be made productive until they died (and their bloodlines died with them). A short-term economic balance could be reached.

DeJarnette lived in pursuit of that balance; he chased it through everything he did. And the physical environment of Western State became his ledger book. This idea is reflected most emphatically in the hospital's production of agricultural goods and DeJarnette's increase of Western State's landholdings to support agricultural labor. The superintendent noted, for example, that 1917 was a particularly good year for agricultural yield, providing 2,400 bushes of peaches, 1,400 barrels of apples, 29,767 gallons of milk, and "all vegetables in abundance." This abundance wasn't just designed to feed the 1,400 patients at Western State that year. It also created a surplus that could be sold for profit to reinvest in the hospital. In 1917, that profit was $17,860. DeJarnette even calibrated the diets of his patients, using food they produced, to ensure maximum affordable nutrition to support this kind of manual labor.

By 1920, the farms, gardens, and orchards were producing what he called an "enormous" yield, including 41,000 pounds of grapes, 19,000 pounds of pork, 35,000 gallons of milk, 125 tons of hay, and 121,748 pounds of cabbage. These commodities translated into $49,644 in profit for the hospital.

In 1926, DeJarnette expanded Western State's landholdings by 252 acres. The $25,000 purchase price was split between the Virginia General Assembly and Western State, with the lion's share of the debt, $16,000, falling to the hospital. But DeJarnette, a man consumed by debt in all its forms, didn't feel trepidation about such a large expense. He noted that with a "few favorable seasons," the new property would pay for itself. The purchase also meant that Western State now controlled its own water basin. In his typical fashion, he meticulously explained how that would benefit the hospital's financial future: "The 6,210,000 gallons per quarter at Staunton rates, 65 cents per 1,000 gallons for the first 35,000; 40 cents for the next 165,000 gallons; 20 cents up to 2,000,000 and 8 cents 2,000,000 amounts to $768.00 per quarter, or $3,072.00 per year, which is the interest on 50,000." To put it in plainer English, control of water meant municipal savings. It also meant the hospital could raise additional livestock that required regular access to potable water.

By 1931, the hospital's farm production amounted to $71,000, which translates to $1,210,858 in today's dollars.

Patients and the farm's animals usually consumed products worth about half of that, and turning fruits and vegetables into canned goods used about another quarter depending on the year. The rest of the money—about 25 percent—became net profit for the hospital. It's not that DeJarnette kept these profits for himself, but he often reinvested a portion back into the agricultural economy by purchasing livestock and machinery and adding structures like barns. For example, by 1931, the farms, gardens, and orchards were producing 65,000 gallons of milk, 36,603 pounds of pork, 56,000 pounds of grapes, 65,932 pounds of cabbage, and an additional fifty other separate commodities like apples, beef, peaches, plums, radishes, squash, strawberries, chickens, and tomatoes.

Western State patients who weren't engaged in agricultural work were made industrious indoors. If you wanted to read a book at the hospital, a patient retrieved it for you. If you needed a door opened, a patient would oblige. Patients cooked and served the food that other patients had harvested. Patients made beds, delivered mail, and shoveled coal into the boiler. If you cut yourself, a patient bandaged you with gauze and dressing that other patients had made. When paint started to peel, a patient touched it up. Every day their hands polished every surface, every floor. If your shoe lost a sole, a patient repaired it. When you died, a patient sewed your burial shroud and put you in the ground.

In 1915, the Virginia State Board of Corrections and Charities published a guide that included an illustration designed to help state leaders understand the innate biological limits of its growing defective and feebleminded population. In it, human progress is depicted as a set of stairs. Men and women struggle and fail to reach the top. The climbers' facial expressions and postures are grim; one woman looks up in despair, a man slumps on his stair. The illustration is meant to help explain a complicated topic: What, exactly, is the difference between an idiot and a high-grade imbecile? Or a low-grade imbecile and a common moron?

The difference, as the illustration explains, is the type of work each category of feebleminded person is able to perform. The lowest step is occupied by the idiot, who is incapable of work. But his neighbor higher up the steps, the low-grade imbecile, can do simple, menial tasks. The medium-grade imbecile and the high-grade imbecile are climbing higher, toward simple and complex manual work. At the top is the moron, who appears to have fallen over in exhaustion, and he is suited for work requiring reasoning. "And so it is with every case," the report explains. "They will not advance mentally. They cannot." These were the people overcrowding Virginia's institutions who could not yet be sterilized, the report lamented. What could be done with them?

The report suggests, "Some authorities, after placing the average economic value of a farm hand at $1.50 a day, and figuring on this basis, have arrived at the conclusion that defectives, excepting idiots, vary in economic value from 30c. to 75c. a day, the general being 54.6c., which is more than the cost of care and maintenance." Virginia could become more aggressive, putting its feebleminded people to work in institutions, which would negate the cost of care and perhaps, the report suggested, even turn a profit.

Virginia's leaders were not alone in this hope. Writing in 1920, Mary T. Waggaman of the US Bureau of Labor Statistics noted several states were showing effective strategies for managing their unfit populations, particularly by "increasing their economic value." As a bonus, Waggaman argued, "domestic and agricultural occupations interest these child grown-ups and make them happy." Out of this desire for greater efficiency, the Lynchburg Colony model of confinement emerged. But other institutions in Virginia struggled to calibrate the elusive balance between minimizing costs and confining large patient populations that included people who had been committed simply on the basis of prejudice toward their race, gender, or class.

Virginia's intention to increase the amount of labor performed at state institutions was aided by a long and overwhelming acceptance of patient work as a therapeutic tool. Francis Stribling, for example, believed work offered patients fresh air, physical activity, and relief from "the excitement of the disease." He encouraged his patients to work in Western's State gardens and on its smaller farm (before Emancipation, enslaved workers performed the hospital's core domestic functions and more physically demanding outdoor work). DeJarnette cited similar benefits, but during his tenure as superintendent, Western State became so reliant on patient labor that it could not function without it. "The number of patients employed during the year averaged 1,001, fifty-five and one-half percent," he wrote in 1931. "Many were exceedingly helpful in the activities of the institution; in fact, our appropriation could not keep the doors of the hospital open were it not for the splendid cooperation in the work of various departments."

This reality was not solely a product of DeJarnette's own preferences. The state did not provide adequate funding for patients. During the last years of DeJarnette's tenure, its annual appropriation for Western State amounted to around $130 to $150 a year per patient. Virginia had also refused to increase hospital workers' wages for decades, which made it difficult for DeJarnette to hire and retain staff. He often advocated for the correction of these issues and did not hesitate to blame the state for what he saw as its mutual failings. He responded to a complaint in 1943 by stating, "I make no claim to proper equipment of the hospital the lack of which has handicapped our work for many years and for which I have pleaded each year in my annual report for funds to supply these needs." DeJarnette actually loathed to see patients working in the hospital by performing patient care themselves. He had radically different views toward skilled and unskilled work. In some instances, he even sometimes reads like a consistent advocate of fair wages for trained staff and even equal pay for women. His wife, for example, was one of the first female psychiatrists licensed in Virginia, although she resigned her position at Western State when they married in 1906. DeJarnette could hold these views at the same time he was extracting profits from patient labor because he did not believe the system itself was coercive. At Western State, he felt the system looked more like the fantasy Waggaman clung to, where childlike grown-ups were grateful for the opportunity to be productive. "Every year strengthens my belief more and more that properly selected and directed employment is the best treatment for the insane," he wrote. "It furnishes diversion and physical tire, both of which are excellent hypnotics."

DeJarnette's disagreements with the state eventually helped end his career as Western State's superintendent. In 1943, a local Episcopal minister, Rev. Carroll Brooke, went public with accusations of patient neglect at the hospital based on conditions he had observed while ministering to patients there. Specifically, he charged that Western State was "run more like a prison than a hospital and that Dr. J. S. DeJarnette, the superintendent, should be persuaded to resign." The wider Staunton community rallied around DeJarnette. The *News Leader* published a collection of letters from local supporters while joining "his legions of friends in hoping that Dr. DeJarnette will see many more years of valuable service." But the state did indeed persuade the seventy-seven-year-old DeJarnette to resign, finding him unfit for duty. Still, he embraced retirement. Some years prior, he had purchased a second home in Staunton as an investment property and was happy to downsize into a smaller life with his wife and favorite niece. He had no children of his own.

Two decades after DeJarnette's retirement, mental health reformers began discussing a phenomenon they observed at state hospitals across the country that they named "institutional peonage." They argued that because patients performed many core duties, from cooking to janitorial work, hospitals had begun to think of them primarily as workers, not patients. Beyond the obvious therapeutic disadvantages of this arrangement, reformers worried that hospitals might confine patients beyond the length of time required for treatment in order to keep utilizing their labor. In a 1964 article for the *Atlantic Monthly*, psychiatrist F. Lewis Bartlett explained:

> State hospitals need "good patients" who are useful, valuable, and expediently indispensable. But these relatively less ill patients, instead of being helped to overcome their illness, as is normally expected on behalf of the patients in any other medical care facility, are doomed by the institutional needs of the state mental health hospital to the pathological dependency characteristics of "good patients."

DeJarnette by no means forced patients to work by explicit order, and nothing suggests he kept any patients confined solely for labor. He didn't need to. For any tasks he considered menial or unskilled, he always had a surplus of workers.

In 1973, the federal government attempted to settle the question of patient labor in one context by ruling in *Souder v. Brennan* that laboring patients should be covered by the Fair Labor Standards Act. The ruling also clarified that the potential therapeutic value of a patient's work was irrelevant.

If a hospital derived economic benefit from patient labor, the activities were protected as work, and this protection included the ability to collect a minimum wage. *Souder* was eventually weakened, but the changes it hoped to produce were intended to work in tandem with other landmark decisions of that decade that defined constitutionally informed baseline standards for the humane care of patients at mental health facilities.

Without the ability to use patient labor, many institutions could no longer sustain the operation of their large facilities, and *Souder* marked a turning point in a larger national trend toward deinstitutionalization. Some historians, like Ruthie-Marie Beckwith, believe that the deinstitutionalization of the 1970s wasn't just about rediscovering the moral center of patient care or better treatments, but a phenomenon that was motivated by legal challenges that threatened the ability of hospitals to manage their workforce by utilizing patient labor.

We might never know the exact economic benefit of the labor patients performed at Western State, although there is value in trying. When patients leveled land for farming, how much value did that add to the price that land claimed at a later date? How many more years of life were provided to the site's fragile architecture by the patients' constant cleaning and polishing? How much did local businessmen save by hiring paroled workers whose value had been mathematically determined to be half the price of another? With patients performing core domestic duties, how much did that deflate the value of paid hospital work? Because landowners knew Western State would be a reliable buyer of land in the area, did that inflate the cost of acreage when it went on the market? What does our own balance sheet look like now?

"The patient is good for work, and work is good for the patient," DeJarnette often wrote. Western State's ledgers were a testament to their industry, but so was the hospital's physical world. Today, though, some traces of this industry might be harder to see than others. The farms are now gone, abandoned by a subsequent generation of superintendents who reduced the hospital's landholdings. The need to transition to more modern facilities intersected with changing attitudes about patient work. Over time, much of the hospital's acreage was sold, repurchased, or swapped between government entities for the development of both newer hospital facilities and commercial enterprises. Now DeJarnette's legacy as a farmer resides mostly in records kept by the Library of Virginia in Richmond, two hours east of Staunton.

DeJarnette's legacy as an architect, though, is something I see every day. He oversaw the construction of seven major buildings at Western State—three physician houses and four institutional buildings. For several of these, including the Wheary Building, he worked off generic architectural plans that he adapted himself. He designed the exteriors to be cohesive with the older architecture, often meaning that many of the same features are present in his buildings, but they look like cheaper copies (because they were). Still, to the untrained eye, his attempts to pass as Thomas Blackburn are sufficient.

DeJarnette admired his architectural creations because, to him, they were pure. They reflected order brought from chaos, but even more, they were monuments to his economic efficiency. The buildings that were built during the DeJarnette era went up under the steam of patient labor at a remarkable savings to the state and the institution. In some cases, it cut the associated costs by half. Patient labor meant DeJarnette could remain in the black, even as his costs were increasing with every new patient who needed to be housed under his management.

Perhaps he looked at the buildings and his frenzied tabulations stopped for a moment. "With the exception of laying the brick practically the whole building is the work of patients, which makes it cost us only the value of the material in it," he wrote of one project. In reports, he often toggles seamlessly between hysterical loathing of the human pollution inflicting their debts on good people and his praise of the goods and buildings the patients produced, talking even sometimes about their "splendid cooperation." There was no contradiction in this for him because the praise was always ultimately for himself. He brought the order. He balanced the ledger. He created purity from the human wreckage whose final elimination he would not live to see. This was his design.

When patients built buildings, the numbers worked and became comforting. Here's DeJarnette describing the construction of new residences for physicians at the hospital:

> A dwelling for one of the assistant physicians has been completed at a cost of $4900. The house is brick, has nine rooms, a large basement, is splendidly arranged and is a valuable addition to hospital property. Had this house been built under contract it would have cost $11,000 to $12,000 but in estimating the cost we do not include patient labor. With the exception of brick work, the construction was done by our regular force.

This regular force did not just perform the brute, physical labor of digging foundations and hauling material, but it also constructed the finer details that DeJarnette says were "splendidly arranged," what architecture specialists call porticos, columns, and transoms. Today, after restoration, these homes are assessed at over $400,000.

DeJarnette was most proud, I think, of the Wheary

Building, which he finished in 1935. Its construction was a complex undertaking. First envisioned as two stories and then extended to three, the Wheary Building is a 45,000-square-foot structure designed with the same emphasis on classical architectural details that carry throughout the hospital complex. Two hundred patients would live there. DeJarnette wanted the building to have the most modern reinforcements and utility systems available, all of them elevated by his best attempt at reproducing the hospital's architectural themes. "I will draw the plans for the building and so save the expense of an architect and construct it with patient labor," he wrote. The building was created to house Western State's suicidal patients. The reinforcements DeJarnette wanted for it were required for their safety and supervision.

At the end of his career, DeJarnette became incredibly defensive about the Wheary Building. He had designed it to project something important that he wanted to claim about his beliefs: that he could be a person who hated the scourge but pitied the patient. He placed additional emphasis on beautifying the structure and believed, despite some of the unusual details required to fit its purpose, that it offered the best accommodation at the hospital. "Of all the sadness and suffering," he wrote in 1931, "those whose hands are turned against themselves and often mutilate themselves in their efforts to liberate their souls from the prison of their bodies. These should have our best accommodation and best efforts."

But DeJarnette was also incensed about the Wheary Building because the patients housed in it were the focus of the complaint Carroll Brooke brought against the hospital that helped end DeJarnette's career. "One of the wards is just a long loft with 140 patients in there all day long and clothes under the bed and clothing scattered all around," Brooke charged. DeJarnette fumed in response:

Although Mr. Brooke claims to be well acquainted with mental sickness and its treatment his course evidentially did not include patients with suicidal tendencies of which we average about 300. 'The long loft' is an ideal fireproof ward for suicidals. Its many windows and wide halls makes it bright, light, and airy for those who by their own unfortunate condition are condemned to confinement and constant observation.

Here, present and past collide again. Brooke and DeJarnette's disagreements about the treatment of patients centers on one section of the Wheary Building they both refer to as "the loft," which is exactly the name Western State developers gave the building in its new life as upscale condominiums.

Whoever Joseph DeJarnette was, whatever Western State was, became this building.

Up on a terraced hillside beside the hospital, beyond the site's last row of structures, is a cemetery. As many as 3,000 patients, people who died indigent or unclaimed by loved ones, are buried there, along with a few members of hospital staff who chose Western State as their final resting place.

Getting to the cemetery from the hotel requires knowing it is there in the first place. There is no signage. In fact, the path to it is marked with several "No Trespassing" signs, and it is barred by a barrier that blocks vehicular traffic. Even though any able-bodied person could just walk around it, I imagine many attempts to visit the cemetery end here out of deference to the rules or private property. Even if someone understands that a cemetery lies on the other side, there are no instructions or signage to explain if access can be granted or how.

When I first moved to Staunton, I incorrectly assumed that developers had not claimed the cemetery land during their deal with the city. I thought, perhaps, that a public entity, state or local, was still caring for it. The alternative seemed too blasphemous to imagine—that, to uncomplicate a real estate transaction, the city simply transformed a public cemetery housing the remains of over 3,000 people into private property. My assumptions were naïve, though. I was thinking with my heart and not my wallet.

After my night at the Blackburn Inn, I walked up to the cemetery in the morning. By visiting the cemetery, I thought maybe I could end my trip with the ability to say that I had found evidence that at least one thing happened for sure during the hundred-year gap in the developers' history of the site: people died. But at Western State, even that's not so simple.

It was sunny and cold, and I had a headache. But no matter—fresh air would be the cure. I reminded myself that I was lucky to be attempting this in colder weather when the overgrowth was thinner. On another visit the previous spring, the ground was softer from wet weather and vegetation straining up toward sunlight, and I almost fell a few times. But that day the going was fairly easy. I walked up the path and down again, past the warning signs, and along the oak trees to a hidden nook.

Three thousand people are buried here, I reminded myself. But there's no way to know who they were or when they died exactly. The markers do not have names or dates, just numbers that correspond to state records, which Virginia argues are confidential. The state will only say that the first burials at the site date from 1848, the last from 2001, and that in between those dates people died. The markers, squat rectangles of concrete and metal laid out in long rows, are worn and broken. The numbers on many of them are no longer legible. Looking at them, you cannot know how many of the dead were men or women, old or young at death, or what their names were.

Because Western State was a segregated hospital for most of the time it operated at this site, we can be certain that the overwhelming number of them were white. But that is all. Mostly the site persists as a cemetery of nameless dead.

Virginia passed a law in 1986 that requires it to use more durable granite for the headstones of indigent burials and to identify the deceased by name and with dates. The state, however, argued it could not use this new law to identify Western State patients. In 2008, a group of former patients formed a coalition to create a more substantial kind of memorial at the cemetery site. The plans didn't progress past the initial idea phase, however. It's possible that, like me, they were slow to understand the cemetery had become private property in 2006.

The morning I was there, it was strange to look at so much neglect after having just left a space where physicians who humanized people with mental illness were lauded as heroes. That space told me their heroism extended from the way they organized the physical world around the need to proclaim that dignity. Here dignity was denied. And who had a part in that? It wasn't just the site's current owners, but the city and state as well.

In my less cozy bed at home that night, I tried again to pinpoint what disturbed me so much about the history of Western State as it was presented by the developers. After all, I could not deny the architectural restoration was sublime. And even though I would say that the developers' version of the site's past was incomplete, I couldn't say it was wrong. I might even concede that the story they tell makes sense. In thinking about places like Western State or Kirkbride Buildings, it *is* possible to stray too far toward the morbid and therefore disadvantage our potential to return the buildings to everyday use. There's an argument to be made, and people like Robert Kirkbride make it, that these sites can still fulfill their original healing purpose by helping communities move forward from dark chapters in their past.

But the city and the site's developers didn't purify Western State of its dark past to help anyone heal; they did it to sell property to rich people. And not just any rich people, but people from afar who are not burdened by any collective stigma about Western State in the first place, but only by the task of finding the perfect second home. *A beautiful home away from home*, the site's marketing suggests, *just like in the past*. That these past homes were often the only ones indigent patients were allowed to know is left unsaid. The only echo of this truth is the neglected cemetery, pocked with erasures, quarantined and rotting.

———————

The philosophies underpinning historic preservation are intended to encourage us to take from the past what we need for the present and future. But what exactly does the redevelopment of Western State Hospital tell us we need now?

In its most basic reading, it tells us about a need to please the wealthiest among us first. It also tells us about a need to justify this orientation by claiming a residual benefit for the rest of us. By virtue of this relationship, however, I become a profiteer without the ability to understand what it is, exactly, that I am profiting from. Is it the arrangement of beautiful historic buildings that have been restored at a considerable cost? Or is it the labor of confined patients that originally built them? It can be both, of course. But the new Western State also tells us our needs will best be met by setting this duality aside.

In a 2015 interview with *CityLab,* Robert Kirkbride noted, "Buildings didn't commit people. People committed people. But it's easier to blame buildings than human behavior." This is accurate. But those buildings are also assets, and their value gets determined, in part, by the residue of human actions that took place within them. The dangers in these old buildings aren't just lead paint and asbestos; they're also the cruel history they can represent. And yet, people don't really seem to "blame buildings" as far as I can tell. Certainly not here in Staunton. Here, the opposite is true—architecture is the thing that redeems Western State's old buildings, diluting their dark history by providing alternative focal points.

Francis Stribling and Joseph DeJarnette both understood that buildings could be an extension of ourselves. The most perfect constructions could even help reconcile all our human contradictions. But what exactly are we trying to reconcile when we reach into the past and start extracting significant economic value from stories about patients who were confined but content, toiling but happy, and banished but dignified? At the very least, we are implying that those contradictions coexisted harmoniously in the past, and that is just not true. *But if they found harmonious coexistence in the past*, we might be in danger of thinking, *why can't they find it also in the present and the future?*

What makes me uncomfortable about Western State's restoration is the permission it grants us to imagine ourselves as people who would have been more likely to ease suffering than to cause or benefit from it. The endurance of the physical world it offers to us proves this. Other details from the hospital's past become transient chapters; brief interruptions in the through line between what we were and who we are. The site's redevelopment invites us to imagine that we've earned our connection to people who treated the most vulnerable with care and dignity. Through the site's beautiful environment, we can experience the pleasure of making a world for the less fortunate without doing it ourselves.

People will ask me, in both good and bad faith, what can be done about this. If it helps, I give my solemn promise not to crash weddings at Western State, complaining about sterilizations and patient labor. I am not calling for the museumification of a commercial development, because that would be a waste of time. I am a realist. The deed is done.

But in a city and state that celebrates the past, would it really be so taxing to live in the truth that the world around us is connected to the lives, labor, and loss of exploited people? That their hands sloped land, made brick, dug foundations, poured concrete, and built assets that, as I write, are still accumulating value? Could we acknowledge that too many of us find it distasteful to admit that buildings designed by a great architect were *built* by people who were enslaved and then later confined within them? Might we talk about how this practice continues today, that Virginia law still mandates the use of prison labor to supply furniture and goods to Commonwealth institutions like public universities? Could we recognize that we are still surrounded by institutions that dehumanize people, not just in far-off detention centers, but here, in our own backyard? Can we be allowed to ask if the new owners of retirement homes at today's Western State will use their political privilege to help make healthcare, and especially mental health care, more accessible for the rest of us? Can we remember that the state executed William Morva, a man with untreated mental illness, not in the distant past but just three years ago? Can we stop pretending that, given the chance, we would have been Francis Stribling, not Joseph DeJarnette?

Because here in the present, right now, we have clear answers to all those questions. We aren't people who can even care for a cemetery.

———

Like Joseph DeJarnette, I am now a person consumed by numbers. As I go through the historical record, I still struggle to comprehend the importance of some of the numbers and figures I find there. Why did Western State list so many young people who were insane one year and then old the next? Why were two people committed there in 1916 because their neighbor died? Who was the person committed the following year who was suffering from both malaria and the symptoms of a "fast life"? How exactly was the hospital able to can 15,000 jars of fruit preserves a year?

The number that I think about most, however, didn't come from DeJarnette's ledger or from any of Western State's records. In a way, it's a number I didn't want to know. By the time I set in motion its discovery, I was already aware that Western State Hospital is the kind of place that inspires uncharitable calculations. I did not want that for myself, and yet all other figures are incomplete without this one.

That number is twenty-eight. That is the number of people since 2015 who have successfully filed a claim to be compensated $25,000 through Virginia's Victims of Eugenic Sterilization Compensation Program. From that number, twenty-eight, we can make a larger one: $700,000. This is how much the regret for fifty-five years of eugenics costs in the state of Virginia.

I try to tell myself that twenty-eight is a good number. It means that Virginia had to pay out more than the $400,000 it originally budgeted when it developed the program, sixty years removed from the era when most of the sterilizations occurred.

But I'm troubled by my own unbalanced ledger. $700,000 is still $500,000 less than the combined tax credits the state of Virginia helped developers to claim for Western State's transformation. It is $249,300,000 less than the total construction costs the developers projected for the site's restoration. It is $20,300,000 lower than the figure developers have provided as their investment in the project to date. If every person who had been sterilized at Western State during DeJarnette's tenure as superintendent—a total he estimated to be 1,205 patients—were still alive and received compensation, their collective payout of $30,125,000 would still be $219,875,000 lower than what investors think the redeveloped property will be worth some day. If all twenty-eight people who have received compensation collectively pooled their money today, they could purchase at most three condominiums at Western State's Villages at Staunton.

I know people will ask me how my own ledger book could ever be balanced. Some of them might even ask me why I keep it. Wouldn't it be better not to? It is done. All of it. They will ask me what good it does to keep talking about these painful things. After all, we will never live in a world where Western State Hospital never happened. When can we say we have earned the right to move on?

My answer is simple: When it is just as easy to give a person a second chance as it is to give one to a building.

SUGGESTED RESOURCES

Baynton, Douglas C. *Defectives in the Land: Disability and Immigration in the Age of Eugenics*. University of Chicago Press, 2016.

Beckwith, Ruthie-Marie. *Disability Servitude: From Peonage to Poverty*. Palgrave Macmillan, 2016.

Bishop, Mary Carter. *Don't You Ever: My Mother and Her Secret Son*. HarperCollins, 2018.

Briggs, Laura. *Reproducing Empire: Race, Sex, Science, and U.S. Imperialism in Puerto Rico*. University of California Press, 2002.

Brown, Molly McCully. *The Virginia State Colony for Epileptics and Feebleminded*. Persea Books, 2017.

Cogdell, Christina. *Eugenic Design: Streamlining America in the 1930s*. University of Pennsylvania Press, 2004.

Cohen, Adam. *Imbeciles: The Supreme Court, American Eugenics, and the Sterilization of Carrie Buck*. Penguin, 2016.

Coleman, Arica L. *That the Blood Stay Pure: African Americans, Native Americans, and the Predicament of Race Identity in Virginia*. Indiana University Press, 2013.

Currell, Sue. "You Haven't Seen Their Faces: Eugenic National Housekeeping and Documentary Photography in 1930s America." *Journal of American Studies* 51(2), 481–511.

Dorr, Gregory Michael. *Segregation's Science: Eugenics and Society in Virginia*. University of Virginia Press, 2008.

Eisenfeld, Sue. *Shenandoah: A Story of Conservation and Betrayal*. University of Nebraska Press, 2015.

Gould, Stephen J. *The Mismeasure of Man*. W. W. Norton & Company, 1981.

Gregg, Sara M. *Managing the Mountains: Land Use Planning, the New Deal, and the Creation of a Federal Landscape in Appalachia*. Yale University Press, 2010.

Holloway, Pippa. *Sexuality, Politics, and Social Control in Virginia, 1920–1945*. University of North Carolina Press, 2005.

Horning, Audrey. *In the Shadow of Ragged Mountain*. Shenandoah National Park Association, 2004.

Kelves, Daniel J. *In the Name of Eugenics: Genetics and the Uses of Human Heredity*. Alfred A. Knopf, 1985.

Kline, Wendy. *Building a Better Race: Gender, Sexuality, and Eugenics from the Turn of the Century to the Baby Boom*. University of California Press, 2001.

Ladd-Taylor, Molly. *Fixing the Poor: Eugenic Sterilization and Child Welfare in the Twentieth Century*. John Hopkins University Press, 2017.

Lambert, Darwin. *The Undying Past of Shenandoah National Park*. Roberts Rinehart, 1989.

Levine, Philippa. *Eugenics: A Very Short Introduction.* Oxford University Press, 2017.

Lombardo, Paul A. *Three Generations, No Imbeciles: Eugenics, the Supreme Court, and Buck v. Bell.* Johns Hopkins University Press, 2008.

McRae, Elizabeth Gillespie. *Mothers of Massive Resistance: White Women and the Politics of White Supremacy.* Oxford University Press, 2008.

Nelson, Louis P. and Claudrena N. Harold (editors). *Charlottesville 2017: The Legacy of Race and Inequality.* University of Virginia Press, 2018.

Nuriddin, Ayah. "The Black Politics of Eugenics." *Nursing Clio,* June 1, 2017.

Ordover, Nancy. *American Eugenics: Race, Queer Anatomy, and the Science of Nationalism.* University of Minnesota Press, 2003.

Parsons, Anne E. *From Asylum to Prison: Deinstitutionalization and the Rise of Mass Incarceration after 1945.* University of North Carolina Press, 2018.

Powell, Katrina M. *"Answer at Once": Letters of Mountain Families in Shenandoah National Park, 1934–1938.* University of Virginia Press, 2009.

Reich, Justin. "Re-creating the Wilderness: Shaping Narratives and Landscapes in Shenandoah National Park." *Environmental History* 6, no. 1 (January 2001): 95-117.

Roberts, Dorothy. *Killing the Black Body: Race, Reproduction, and the Meaning of Liberty*. Vintage Books, 1997.

Robinson, Richard Knox (director). *Rothstein's First Assignment*. Cinema Guild, 2011.

Rose, Sarah F. *No Right to Be Idle: The Invention of Disability, 1840s–1930s*. University of North Carolina Press, 2017.

Saini, Angela. *Superior: The Return of Race Science*. Beacon Press, 2019.

Schoen, Johanna. *Choice and Coercion: Birth Control, Sterilization, and Abortion in Public Health and Welfare*. University of North Carolina Press, 2005.

Sherman, Shantella Yolanda. *In Search of Purity: Popular Eugenics and Racial Uplift Among New Negroes 1915–1935*. CreateSpace Publishing, 2016.

Smith, David J. and K. Ray Nelson. *The Sterilization of Carrie Buck*. New Horizon Press, 1999.

Stepan, Nancy Leys. *The Hour of Eugenics: Race, Gender, and Nation in Latin America*. Cornell University Press, 1996.

Stern, Alexandra Minna. *Eugenic Nation: Faults and Frontiers of Better Breeding in Modern America*. University of California Press, 2015.

Tayac, Gabrielle. "Eugenics and Erasure in Virginia: Walter Plecker's War Against Virginia's Tribes." *National Museum of the American Indian Magazine* (February 2009): 20–24.

Torpy, Sally J. "Native American Women and Coerced Sterilization: On the Trail of Tears in the 1970s." *American Indian Culture and Research Journal* 24(2): 1–22.

Trombley, Stephen (director). *The Lynchburg Story: Eugenic Sterilization in America*. Channel Four and Filmmakers Library, 1994.

ARCHIVAL RESOURCES

This book utilized archival collections held by the Library of Virginia (Richmond), the University of Virginia Special Collections (Charlottesville), and the Augusta County Historical Society (Staunton). In addition to these, a number of digital resources were also enormously helpful, including the Eugenics Archive (eugenicsarchive.ca), maintained through the Social Sciences and Humanities Research Council of Canada. Georgia State University College of Law, through Paul Lombardo, also maintains a digital reading room of eugenics legal matter and important documents related to *Buck v. Bell.* The HathiTrust Digital Library and the Internet Archive allowed me to more easily locate and read contemporary eugenic texts. Below is a brief selection of these texts.

Cox, Earnest Sevier. *White America,* 1925.

Davenport, Charles B. *Heredity in Relation to Eugenics,* 1911. See also Davenport, "Eugenic Sterilization in Virginia" in *Virginia Medical Monthly* (January 1931).

Dugdale, Richard. *The Jukes: A Study in Crime, Pauperism, Disease, and Heredity,* 1877.

Estabrook, Arthur H. and Ivan E. McDougle. *Mongrel Virginians: The WIN Tribe,* 1926.

Galton, Francis. *Hereditary Genius,* 1869.

Goddard, Henry H. *The Kallikak Family: A Study in the Heredity of Feeblemindedness,* 1912.

Grant, Madison. *The Passing of the Great Race: Or, the Racial Basis of European History*, 1916.

Jordan, David Starr. "The Blood of the Nation: A Study in the Decay of Races by the Survival of the Unfit," in *Popular Science* (May 1901).

Laughlin, Harry H. *The Legal Status of Eugenical Sterilization: History and analysis of litigation under the Virginia Sterilization Statute, which led to a decision in the Supreme Court of the United States upholding the statute*, 1930.

Powell, John. *The Breach in the Dike: An Analysis of the Sorrels Case Showing the Danger to Racial Integrity from Intermarriage of Whites with So-Called Indians*, 1925.

Stoddard, Lothrop. *The Rising Tide of Color: Against White World Supremacy*, 1922.

ACKNOWLEDGMENTS

Acknowledgments are typically written to recognize the valuable labor and support of individuals and institutions that contributed to the writing process. This recognition will follow, but before that, I want to use this space to make other declarations that embrace the other meaning of "acknowledgment," that of an acceptance of truth.

I am writing this in a moment that is filled with eugenic ideas surrounding the United States' management of the COVID-19 crisis. The worst consequences of COVID-19 are suffered disproportionately by Black, brown, and Native peoples, poor people, disabled people, and the elderly. To the indifferent public and leaders chafing under their own inabilities, this suffering is acceptable. These victims, their actions imply, were not worth protecting and they had no right to expect a duty of care. Those who recovered quickly from COVID-19 and those who haven't yet been infected are often framed as biologically "better" than the stricken and the dead. Every cold question contained in this book, every frame of reference for determining the relative worth of a human's life, are now, as ever, informing the logic of the powerful in naked and craven ways.

Blaming our weak and ineffective national response on the Trump administration is both low-effort and incomplete. This crisis belongs to the White House, but it also belongs to anyone who derives pleasure, profit, or power from a system that demands people be productive or passively killed. It belongs to bosses and business owners who need to be reminded with the force of law that their workers are real people; it belongs to politicians of all stripes who oppose highly popular material changes, like universal healthcare, that would improve our lives immeasurably. This moment also belongs to the callousness of ordinary people who look at the lives led by people on the margins and find ways to blame their hardships on unspecified weakness, leveraging self-directed myths of exceptional worthiness to explain society's winners and losers. It belongs to anyone satisfied with the rationing of resources, believing that deprivation is a useful form of coercion.

The United States has experienced more than 120,000 COVID-19 deaths, and as I write, a large and vocal segment of the public recites pseudoscience to justify human loss through the ghoulish and often speculative presentment of preexisting conditions, disabilities, lifestyle choices, and the advanced ages of victims. Fitter Americans will survive, politicians like Texas Lieutenant Governor Dan Patrick assured us in March, and perhaps even thrive once the frail are culled. In writing this book, I struggled to formulate concise and relatable ways of explaining how eugenics, in its twentieth-century iteration, could have become overwhelmingly popular among scientists and laypeople alike, how people could have heard and embraced these ugly ideas without flinching, believing their souls would remain intact. This moment has unburdened me from that chore.

I am grateful for the support of Belt Publishing, including publisher and founder Anne Trubek, senior editor and marketing director Martha Bayne, associate publisher Dan Crissman, and orders and fulfillment manager William Rickman. Once again, I have been exceedingly fortunate to work with David Wilson and Meredith Pangrace on visual and cover design. An extended note of thanks is due to Michael Jauchen, who served as this book's primary editor. Mike's thoughtful and generous work improved this book from its earliest versions to its final proofing, and I am tremendously appreciative of his efforts. Much of this work took place during a pandemic and amid the worst economic crisis in modern history, and I am proud to be affiliated with a publishing team that centered the safety and well-being of staff and authors in the readjustments made necessary by these two concurrent crises.

This book would not be possible without the scholarly and archival labor of others, including the experts cited throughout the text and in the back matter, and the institutional staff at the Library of Virginia and the University of Virginia Special Collections. The labor of archival workers is often invisible, and I recognize the tremendous effort and skill required to arrange collections and produce findings aids that lighten the research process. I am especially grateful to Suzanne Fisher at the Augusta County Historical Society. Suzanne has worked extensively with a collection of personal papers and ephemera related to Joseph DeJarnette, and she volunteered her time outside of operating hours to assist me. I am also grateful to Alison Bell at Washington and Lee University for sharing her work on asylum cemeteries, including the cemetery at Western State, and for introducing me to a cohort of scholars who are currently studying the history of eugenics in Virginia. Many thanks also to public historian Perri Meldon, who shares my interest in questions of land, space, and the interpretation of the eugenic past. I am so appreciative of her comradery and willingness to chat about readings and topics that are often heavy and unsettled.

The largest debt is owed to my partner Josh Howard. No one has or will ever do more than this good human being. Thank you.